NORMAL'S JUST A CYCLE
ON A WASHING MACHINE

Enjoy!
Len B

Len Bourland

EPB PUBLISHING
Dallas, Texas

EPB Publishing, LLC

8225 Chadbourne Rd

Dallas, Texas 75209

www.lenbourland.com

First printing, September 2016

ISBN 978-0-9977415-0-6

ISBN 978-0-9977415-1-3 e-book

Library of Congress Control Number 2027076345

Bourland, Len Persons

Normal's Just a Cycle on a Washing Machine

Cover by Courtney Barrow

Formatting by PhotoLively, LLC

Table of Contents

NORMAL'S JUST A CYCLE ON A WASHING MACHINE

Dedicated to my grandchildren
Ella, Margo, Caroline, Julia,
Walter and James

Preface

Thirty years ago before SUVs, kids used to pile into the back of station wagons for field trips without notarized forms or seat belts, "criss cross Indian style, don't touch your neighbor." Students rode their bikes without helmets, carpooling moms sipped home-brewed coffee long before Starbucks, pets roamed the neighborhood without leash laws, and nannies were rare. There were no cell phones or Internet, and most families could find mom in the kitchen at five o'clock actually cooking on the stove while walking around talking on the phone attached to the wall with a long cord, peering out the window at children, making notes with other mothers to co-ordinate events for the morrow. My kids researched their homework in grade school using our encyclopedia. We wrote letters on stationery with licked on stamps. It is in this world I proposed a column idea, not unlike the college column I wrote for the *Nashville Tennessean* as a Vanderbilt co-ed, "Campus Capers." The fledgling *Park Cities People*, a suburban weekly, accepted my proposal for

"Carpool Capers" which quickly morphed into wider subject matter.

In this halcyon world the Christmas list for Santa included a Cabbage Patch doll and a new invention that was the pre-cursor to video games, Intellevision. My husband and I debated whether to get Beta or VHS for our TV to enjoy the newest phenomenon, the video store. We went with VHS because our new video camera, which was the size of a small canon, used VHS tapes to film our young kids. The single greatest change of the last generation has, arguably, been technology. I wrote my first columns on an IBM selectric typewriter with a new gizmo that could erase up to five letters without having to use liquid paper. Using selections of my columns over time, it becomes apparent that life could be anything but the relentlessly upbeat Mayberry portrayed in the early years of my column writing dubbed "Pre-Soak." The paper changed ownership, publishers, editors, and formats many, many times, and so did my voice.

The French are right with their maxim, "the more things change the more they remain the same." Early on we didn't have laptops crashing and cell phones, but we still had "the dog ate my homework" syndrome, picky eaters, teenagers sneaking out, holiday crazies, traffic, over and under involved parents; in short, life as we still know it. These years are reflected in Part Two, "Normal Wash." Yet even as I began to get writing awards for my column, *At Our House*, my happy housewife world imploded in my forties as reflected in Part Three, "Spin Cycle." Highland Park, Texas has often been dubbed "The Bubble." Well, one year my bubble burst.

Both my life and society changed very rapidly as did my children going through adolescence, when I become a single working mother…who dates. Enter the New Normal and the New Millennium with Part Four, "Second Wash," which encompasses the world at large, from emerging cell phones and the Internet to 9/11 to my nest emptying with romances all around.

"Turbo Spin" and "Gentle Wash" are very brief conclusions, which take the reader full cycle, although there is, undoubtedly, always Wash, Spin, Repeat in life. Most of these columns have been excerpted, occasionally two combined, but all have been published in the years listed; several were read on KERA on NPR. My own thoughts to propel the narrative have been italicized, while what has already appeared in print is in standard type.

The impetus for this book was the phone call a few years ago from my oldest, closest friend with her terminal diagnosis. How could it be possible that we baby boomers who came of age in the radical 60s could be dying in our 60s? This clear-eyed raven beauty had been the motherly big sister I had never had. She came to campus from Texas in bold purples and pinks, while we Atlanta girls still wore icky poo pastel shirtwaist dresses, with matching hair bows. She got me through theory calculus in college (barely), and we sat late into the night in the dorm as we discussed everything from Siddhartha to Shakespeare. Our worlds rapidly changed with political assassinations, anti-war and civil rights protests everywhere, the Motown sound transitioning to psychedelic music, and our hemlines going up while our hair got longer. The summer of the moonwalk we cavorted through Europe skirting hippies and student revolutions. When her baby came and she made me godmother, I was thrilled to respond by having her as my matron of honor the following year. Just a few years later, she welcomed me and my new babies to Dallas, helping me find a house, a pediatrician, babysitters...the works. While geography

4

soon separated us, we always stayed close. She arrived at my door every time my life cracked apart. When she gracefully transitioned out of this world–too soon– it was clear to me she had been put on this planet to delight us all.

And me? We are all terminal, but after her diagnosis I wondered what regrets or unfinished business I would have if I knew my endgame. Taking leave of such a special person gave me the deadline to write the book, a collection of my best columns, that I had postponed for so long. So I began to search for and assemble all those newspaper columns I had never saved, and it took months. Sifting through hundreds of columns, I wondered how to make sense out of my life. I both laughed and cried going back through all those years. My original idea for a collection of popular essays evolved into my own story as told through various life cycles. Maybe my task on this planet is to remember.

In more than a trip down memory lane, my hope is that the reader will enjoy washing and sorting the laundry of my life with yours and society at large by glancing through columns from the optimistic Reagan Era 80s until whatever these years are now. Highland

Park and surrounding neighborhoods centered on family, school, church, vacations, sports, work, and politics with a gumbo of people who can range from the angelic to the annoying.

Meet me with my family as we were joining the up and comers while trying to figure out how to do family values in the land of flash and cash, which is now pretty much the way it is everywhere. Yet for all the consumerism, this a community also filled with big Texas *howdies*. It makes me chuckle.

It is a rare woman who does not face a crisis at some point. When it involves not only herself but also her nest, it can be bewildering and overwhelming, trying to figure out how to mop up and move on. Forging a new life never planned for or envisioned is my story. Cycling back to living in a world that makes me laugh is my journey. I still get the occasional traffic ticket as detailed in my initial column. My (grown) kids and theirs still never let me forget it.

PRE-SOAK

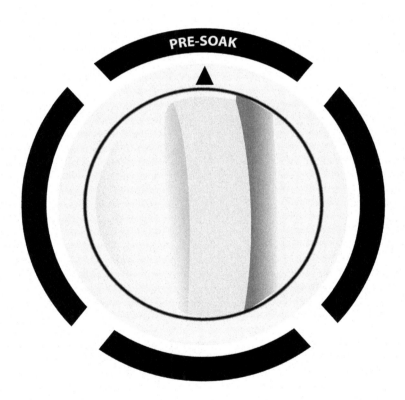

Part One: Pre-Soak

So begin the sunny days of moving to Dallas with a young family to our first home as professionals. I'm finally past the salad days–green, young, and peak– of being a struggling mother, teaching pre-school and going to graduate school, seemingly always barefoot and pregnant. Living on a shoestring while having no time, no money, and dealing with my wildly dysfunctional parents was my norm. This, even as my college sweetheart husband trained around the clock for nine looooong years. Out of our twenties and into our thirties, we are launched into the world of adults who are getting and spending and raising a family. We love our neighborhood and our first "grown-up" house. I pick up my pen for the local suburban weekly, a family friendly community rag.

Spring 1984, *Carpool Capers* (*Meet mommy me getting a traffic ticket*)

If you drive the same carpool routes for enough years, enough times a day, it's bound to happen in our highly patrolled bedroom communities–the traffic ticket. This never happens on the way to pick up a carpool, no matter how late you are or how fast you're cautiously flying to face the wrath of six angry kids who will scowl and yell, "You're Late!" Cops sense this urgency and look the other way. It's on the way home with a packed car that the speed traps are set. And well, ticket quotas are ticket quotas.

Armed with this prior knowledge I shouldn't have been too surprised last week when the motorcycle pulled out from behind a brick wall, red lights flashing to the whoops of the preschoolers.

A black mood descends on an already beaten-down mom. An animated babble erupts throughout the car as each child details every ticket his mom has ever gotten. I am somewhat cheered as my misery needs company. I knew I would hear about this in carpool lines and on soccer fields for weeks. "Well, kids be sure to tell your moms there is a policeman here," I tossed out. "Oh my mom knows already," one little guy piped up. As nonchalantly as I could I asked what happened. My officer was having none of my plea for a warning as he handed me the ticket. "Oh she does what she does every time. She cried," he rejoined. She still got the ticket I was informed. I was feeling better all the time.

Spring 1984, ***Shooting the Bird*** *(Here are the kids)*

We had conference day recently...that's a day when you go to school to hear from the teacher in about five minutes what you already suspected. Then you have the rest of the day to spend with your kids with only two weeks left before summer vacation. This gives you a foretaste of summer and a mild anxiety attack. As I surveyed my two sons ages nine and eleven blowing Hubba Bubba and listening to "California Girls" (it's back), reading comic books and looking bored, they asked to go shoe shopping on this rainy day. From the recesses of my mind I conjured up a recent headline in a news magazine, "Has America Gone Soft?" Was I raising another two little consumers for the next generation? Then Fate took over.

My five-year-old daughter came running in screaming that there was a real live bird flying around in the living room. I did the mature adult thing. I also screamed, picked her up and barricaded us in my bedroom, frantically trying to find pest control in the Yellow Pages. After all I had been raised on Alfred Hitchcock's horror movie, *The Birds* and am no fool. Quickly my boys sprang into action. They rummaged through their closets emerging in full camouflage regalia complete with helmets and BB guns. To be able to have indoor target practice, legally, was irresistible and the firing went on for some time. I was kept informed and soon the triumphant warriors emerged with one very dead bird. Not since Bonnie and Clyde has a living creature taken on so much shot. As I was cleaning up residual bird mess, a cadre of neighborhood troops appeared to survey the scene and go out into the rain to bury the bird.

I contemplated the youth of our country. Soft? I think we're safe if combat readiness is any indicator. America. Love it or leave it.

August 1984, *In the Swim* (The Bubble…Highland Park)

It's a clear crisp morning, actually more like the crack of dawn at 6:30 a.m. I hum pleasantly as I drive to SMU for the big day; it's the Friday that everyone knows about but does not actually discuss because then her child might not get in! It's the sign-up for summer swim lessons, the best swim lessons around. Last year, I had arrived at 8:30 for an 8 a.m. registration thinking I'd skip the lines only to have an officious woman boom "Honey, classes have been long closed. The only thing left is advanced diving in late July." My stomach, however, began churning when the sign on the door read, "Doors open at 5 a.m." Really? After all this wasn't exactly camping out for tickets at a rock concert. It was worse. Half of town was sprawled on sleeping bags with thermoses of coffee, talking or reading newspapers. When I spotted two Junior League Ball Chairmen without their makeup, I knew I was sunk. Glumly I got number #146.

At 7:45 an athletic man came in and blew a whistle; the polite buzzing ceased and we were moving. Ok, ok, I told myself, don't panic. Of course you won't get May or even early June. Pray for late June because we're going out of town in July. I madly picked out my first six choices and had my check ready. As part of the "latecomers," those over number 100, my first four choices had closed out, the man in front of me got my fifth but I CLOSED OUT THE LAST EARLY JUNE NOVICE II SECTION! Not only had I gotten my kids in a class but also I had arrived at the late hour of 6:30. I smiled sympathetically at those bewildered souls who were just coming in the door at 7:55.

What is the lesson of all of this? If having motivated parents means anything then I guess we have future Olympians on our hands. I cannot imagine my mother going though any of this. How do you sign up for next year? Hmmm, I dunno. Uh, really can't quite remember. I guess…just ask around…

September 1984, *Marriage–American Style (Here's the hubby)*

As another anniversary in my marriage has come and gone, it has occurred to me that with the wisdom of over a dozen years experience, I now hold certain truths too be self-evident about the institution:

• That the harmony of a marriage is in direct proportion to the amount of closet space in a house.

• That if you don't paint, repair, redecorate or remodel any portion of your dwelling before you move in, you'd better learn to live with it.

• That you can never send a husband to a store of any kind and have him return with only those items on the list. (A corollary to this is that after he's been to the store several times to "help you out" and there's too much month left at the end of the money, he'll want to know why you can't stick to a budget.)

• That if he's not home by 7:30 at night, it would be better for him to wait until after little ones are fast asleep and not just getting sent to bed.

• That the longest distance between two points is from

where he parks the car and the front door of the restaurant, movie etc.

• That he'll always remember to pull out your chair…if his mother is around.

• That old Eagle scouts still know how to leave a trail… of shoes, socks, newspapers, towels… leading to the bed.

•That he'll always relinquish the wheel on road trips… after the kids are asleep in the back.

•That after years of washing his socks, eating his barbeque, listening to the same repertoire of jokes and anecdotes, boosting him up when he's down, cheering him on when he's up (and vice versa), that love doesn't mean never having to say your sorry, it means never having to say anything at all. Like the subject of the imperative sentence, it's the understood you.

Summer 1984, *More Carpool Capers (Finally a new car)*

The old yellow wagon had nearly 100,000 miles on it, and I'd complained about it for at least three and a half of the last seven years. The radio had long since quit, which made my car very uncool with the carpool set. The knob on the driver's window had dropped off somewhere along the line, so that at the inevitable toll booth a quick performance was impossible; thus my car always finished last on museum field trips. I had ruined several items of clothing on the little wire that poked out of the seat on my side, and last winter I'd become a master at using a metal nail file to prop open the choke under the hood on cold mornings. (Actually my sons were fairly impressed by this.) Clearly it was time for a new model.

But that car was a history of my parenting. I'd gone to the hospital three times and come home with three very special gifts. Moreover, that car was finely seasoned with the aroma of years of decomposing French fries between the cracks in the seats. How many shakes had tumped over? Like a pair of old comfortable shoes this car was going to be difficult to part with. When my firstborn threw up after he had tubes in his ears, no one worried about the car. When my second tossed his gum out the window on a beach trip and it blew back on the window, we all just laughed. When we took a carload of sticky fingered three-year-old little girls home from a birthday party, we weren't thinking about the upholstery.

When it came time to clean her up to take to the dubious dealer for a trade-in, we had another history lesson. Stuffed in a hole in the torn upholstery in the ceiling were all sorts of treasures: coins, crayon nubs,

Happy Meal prizes. In the seat cracks we found one lost Cub Scout patch, cause for much jubilation, an earring I'd lost, and a credit card we'd never missed.

We love our new van although friends forget to wave because I'm not in an old yellow station wagon. There are new electric windows, the radio works great and I'm even starting to learn a few new tunes. But I just gritted my teeth when a coke got knocked over yesterday and the soccer team tramped in mud. It's not quite "home" just yet. It takes time.

January 1985, *The Snowball Effect (Now here's the dog)*

We just got a new puppy. He fits right in with our family: he's small, yaps a lot, and is a picky eater. I didn't realize this would be a social event, but he has nearly had his fur rubbed off from all the love. Every kid in the neighborhood has been through at least twice, sometimes with relatives. There is something touching about a new pup; even the stoniest faces break into a grin when confronted by those liquid black eyes in a fluffy white face. Hence the name Snowball, aka "Snowy" or to my sons "Balls."

This week I've got my work cut out for me. He's

been invited to all three kids' classes, has to get shots at the vet, and I must run around town to get chew toys, bedding, not to mention a special (pricey) dog food as that, it seems, is all he will eat. The neighbors, who had this litter, assure me he must get registered. It seems we have an exotic breed that my asthmatic can tolerate, a Bichon Frise, with bloodlines. I'm sleep deprived from staying up all night with a crying puppy, and friends inform me I need to line up the exterminator or we will have a flea problem. Then a groomer is in order, as this little variety needs to be groomed every six weeks. I don't even get groomed that much. Cheap this dog is not.

There's a silver lining here. The theory goes that after a few years dogs and their owners resemble each other. Maybe by the time I turn 40 I'll look as good as the dog!

Fall 1985, Press release: Writer/Mother Bourland gets new column *(Goody!)*

By popular demand writer Len Bourland has been given her own column which will appear every other week…The column entitled *At Our House* will examine the joys and frustrations of being a wife and mother in today's world. Bourland's wry sense of humor and clever storytelling have earned her a local following. Bourland, a self-described "child of the corporate move" was born in New Orleans and has lived in Houston; Atlanta; Nashville; Jackson, Mississippi; Sao Paulo, Brazil; and lives with her husband, a surgeon. "After four years of med school and five years of residency which made St. Elsewhere look tame, I can safely say it's no weekend date…but he's the finest guy I know and my best friend." Together they have three children.

NORMAL'S JUST A CYCLE ON A WASHING MACHINE

NORMAL

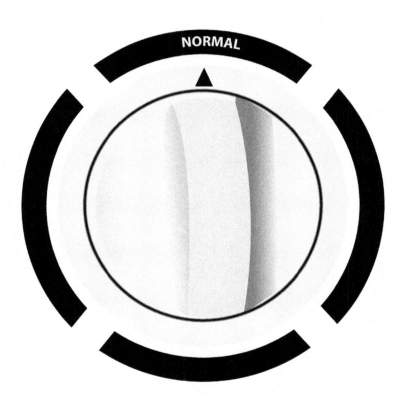

NORMAL'S JUST A CYCLE ON A WASHING MACHINE

Part Two: Normal Wash (At Our House)

Fall 1990, Press release: Park Cities' Column airs on radio show

Len Bourland, longtime columnist has been named a radio commentator for KERA (90.1 FM)

And so my minor following expands from readers in the most Republican zip code on the planet to my younger more Democratic listeners on National Public Radio's local morning drive time. I broadcast about everything from cockroach remedies to Ebonics. Life is busy, happy and fun. My family is in the prime of life.

Spring 1986, *The Fort (Snips and snails and puppy dog tails)*

In this age of 55 foot lots and video games, it might be argued that city boys are handicapped in their youth—that they will never enjoy the nostalgic days of their fathers and grandfathers who knew the idylls of sandlot ball and fishing down by the swimming hole or creek. Even before the clubhouse scene in the popular film *Stand By Me*, my boys, aged 11 and 12 invented a

23

new way to pass gloomy winter and rainy spring days. They discovered the garage, or rather the eaves of it.

Every boy craves a hideaway from the civilization of a room, which is subject to scrutiny and cleaning. My boys have long been connoisseurs of "alley hunting," exploring the discarded remains of our neighborhood proving the old maxim that one man's trash is another man's treasure. Over the years I have been stupefied at the origins of scuffed up briefcases, old hunting clothes, mangled tennis racquets and the like. As I noticed swarms of pre-pubescent males in our garage, I found the answer to an alley scavenger's dream and the neighborhood subterfuge. As every Englishman has his club, every Archie Bunker his chair, my boys have a nook over the rafters planked with found lumber. The only way up is a rope ladder let down for members only: males, no curious girls. I sent my husband up to inspect for safety and "contraband," but upon descent he pronounced it grubby but safe and was frankly a little envious.

A bucket and pulley serve to haul up the necessary rations of Cheetos and root beer. Members must phone up through the communications system of a piece of old hose dangling down. Carpet squares, old pillows, and one broken lawn chair furnish the inner sanctum. A battery-powered fan operated from an old erector set provides ventilation.

As I pass by the garage with a sack of trash on my way to the alley, I can sometimes pick up snatches of conversation including expletives, which is where that kind of language belongs, in the nether realms of a secret hideaway far away from Mom. As I sit at the window folding clothes and watching a gaggle of boys give the secret knock and surreptitiously creep into the garage, I wish somewhat wistfully for a little private nook of my own.

Somehow the laundry room just doesn't cut it.

Summer 1986, *Highland Park Housewives Can Do It All (Bubble-ettes)*

Last Week my fractious aging Chevy van would not crank in the driveway. Overheated? Fortunately, my driveway was contiguous to my neighbor's and her brand new Cadillac with its brand new jumper cables was aligned with my van. Because it was a weekday and only women and children were around, no menfolk, that genre that knows innately how to burp, throw a ball and jump start a car, my neighbor and I decided that as empowered women we could figure this out. Good old school teachers that we had been, we got out the instructions and were attempting to figure out whether it was black to black or red to black on hookups when we read "CAUTION! Batteries contain acid, which can explode. Wear protective clothing!" So we adjourned and came back in long sleeves, shower caps, swim goggles, bandanas over our mouths like the Lone Ranger, and Playtex rubber gloves.

By this time the crowd of neighborhood boys had gathered with the pre-school little sisters hovering as the word "pyrotechnics" had spread down the block. We moved the children back several yards and resumed our mission. We poured over the manual. Black to red, right? We had bogged down again over whether to start the engines first and then connect the cables or vice versa, when a yardman cutting the grass across the street sauntered over and asked, "Uh, you ladies need some help?"

What was his clue? With complete relief we handed over the cables to a disappointed crowd.

Forevermore, the males in my family will pass by a stranded car and say, "Wow, there's somebody jumping off a car without a shower cap on."

April 1987, *Of Mouthwash and Hair Mousse*
(Tweenage)

There are basically two kinds of families: those who share bathrooms and those where each family member has his own facility. We belong to the former category; we know each other well at our house. I can get in and out of the bathroom (shower, apply makeup while mopping up the floor with one foot and a soggy towel and buttoning the back of a first grader's dress) in under five minutes. I have always been baffled by those magazine articles with titles like "Twelve tips for speeding up your makeup regimen to just five minutes!" I have no idea what some women do that takes that long. But then nobody has ever asked me for my beauty secrets either.

Who has five whole minutes before noon anyway? Well, actually my two pre-teen sons seem to. They can spend endless amounts of time on their morning ablutions behind locked doors, especially on cotillion days, gargling, and depressing cans of lots of things going "pssssst."

We have a bluish tint to our lips from breathing oxygen depleted by an ozone layer that has been saturated by the fluorocarbons of the cosmetics industry. The rhetorical question you're asking is why I allow all this goop in the house when I know it in no way compensates for IQ points, personality and at best has a marginal effect on the looks of budding middle-schoolers. It is the age of the shaky ego, and mothers go to great lengths, including abbreviated personal time in the bathroom, so that all kids can get to a mirror to start the day looking good to the world (their friends).

Of course, since the mirror only serves as a magnifying glass to their physical imperfections, real or imagined, this can be, in fact always is, a time-consuming and emotional experience. It is only the insistent pounding of siblings on the bathroom door that gets everyone to breakfast. It has come to me in one of my mini-shower epiphanies that at the exact time in life when as parents we have a sense of who we are and don't really care what anyone thinks, that our children have entered the age of anxiety, seeking approval from their friends…even though they're not totally sure who their friends actually are. Sigh.

Summer 1987, *Off the Market* (*The house not me*)

It took less than a year in what was termed a "tough market," but we finally sold our house. No more yelling, "Man your battle stations" as a couple on their way out of town just had to pop in at five o'clock while I was trying to cook tacos. No more keeping leaf and lawn bags handy to scoop up everything that was not furniture, stuff it in the car along with the dog and circle the block as a family nosed through our cabinets and cupboards. No more putting out plants in unlikely places like bathrooms and potting pansies for the front stoop and lining up our shoes like little soldiers in every closet. No more hanging out in public places like parks and movies on Sunday afternoons so the realtor could hold an open house.

There was the weekend when my agent was out of town and we were enjoying a Sunday of well-deserved respite, reverting to type; the boys were watching *Revenge of the Nerds* while slovenly eating popcorn and my daughter was bandaging all her Barbies with toilet paper in the powder room with the predictable result when too much paper lands in the toilet. Surveying the scene I went for a walk.

Upon my return my husband informed me that a couple had stopped by, knocked on the door and pleaded to run through the house because "we don't care what it looks like at all." Only a man would fall for that line. He mumbled something about their not staying long. I'm far from a member of the white glove set, but there is something too personal about having strangers see where the intimacies of daily living transpire. It's being stripped bare somehow. But the worst is over. We've sold and bought and boxed up. Did I mention we're going to remodel?

November 1987, *Say Cheese! (Just oneeeee picture around the tree)*

There is nothing that produces indigestion after the holiday feast quite like that one inevitable line, "Now I want everybody together for just one family picture." My kids immediately leap for the great outdoors knowing it will take at least 30 minutes before 18 or so people can be assembled, cameras adjusted, hair coiffed, babies changed, furniture rearranged, and kids harnessed. Invariably once the clan is assembled, children sense the vulnerability of the adults and many power plays ensue. A two-year-old will throw a tantrum, a sullen teenager refuses to tuck in his shirt or get his hair out of his eyes, and a charming ten-year-old feels the need to pass gas. My kids usually accept cold, hard cash. It is no mystery to me why the pros can charge hefty fees. The tension mounts in these little family dramas until the rosy cheeks on the adults is bottled rage.

Zoom in on any family shot and notice that people are not so much smiling as baring teeth. Mothers are not so much encircling their toddlers with loving arms as tethering them in the picture. Fathers' arms are not so much resting on their sons' shoulders as pressing them down with white knuckles. Look past the obvious relative caught blinking and you might spot baby spit-up on the mother's shoulder or a pair of mismatched socks on a kid.

Having just spent the afternoon and three rolls of film chasing my own three around the backyard trying to capture three pleasant expressions for a Christmas card, I'm using the shot of the three in the bottom right hand corner of the photo with a large expanse of sky. The sky is actually fairly lovely. I think it's appropriate my 13-year-old's mouth is covered by his sister's ponytail. We spend the majority of the day trying to cover his mouth anyway. My twelve-year-old looks sullen but the rabbit ears he makes over his sister's head attest to his sparkling wit. She is in the Christmas top I made that she hates, but she is two dollars richer for the wearing.

I have already received several Christmas cards with children in multiple hand-smocked outfits smiling in front of a decorated mantle. I take malicious pleasure in knowing it took that poor mother about 150 hours to get that one moment on film. I'm getting too old for this kind of pressure, plus my kids are getting past the darling age anyway. Next year no photo card but I know exactly what I'm going to write inside the card. Peace

December 24 1987, *Christmas De-Lights (Just a teensy bit of stress)*

We've baked Christmas cookies for the neighbors, delivered spiced tea to friends and teachers, mailed Christmas cards with the kids in their Halloween outfits, and even had the usual battle over hanging Christmas lights. Perhaps a little reader input could settle the annual light debate at our house. True or False:

•Blinking lights are more attractive than static ones (T F)

•Large lights are more festive than small twinkle lights (T F)

•All white lights are prettier than colored lights (T F)

•It's OK to hang a really huge string of lights on the tree even if half is shorted out, if you put the burned out part at the back of the tree. (T F)

If you answered true to these questions you can spend next Christmas with my husband. If you answered False you have great taste. The same people who like big colored blinking lights probably also like flocked trees instead of the natural green of a freshly bought tree. It never ceases to amaze me that my husband, a man who was brought up in the Deep South, wants our tree to look like it was cut down and brought inside in the middle of a blizzard. I believe this quiz on Christmas preferences is essential to marital harmony and should be included by all clergy in pre-nuptial counseling.

But the warmth and love of Christmas is a process not a day. So relax and enjoy. That's what we do at our house. (Our house is the one with the large blinking white lights over the front door, and the tree in the window with small colored lights and the one dark place where the lights are burned out.)

June 1988, *Remodeling (A bit more of that stress thing)*

There are a few unforgettable times in life...like the time I thought I had the flu with an eight-month-old baby, only it wasn't the flu, it was morning sickness. Or the time I shakily came home from taking my three- year-old daughter to have her first set of stitches in her chin, and she tripped coming in the door and burst every one which took us right back to the hospital. Or like this week when the chem can and dempster dumpster returned to our property to complete remodeling.

We thought we could live with our old galley kitchen a few years longer; but when the second eye on the old stove went out, the dishwasher did little more than dampen the dishes, the door fell off the pantry and we just left it there, and we could either have cold food in the refrigerator or ice in the freezer compartment but not both with that thermostat, we just bit the bullet. It was time to call the contractor when the kitchen began to resemble the one in my husband's old frat house. We know we're fortunate to live in a nice neighborhood, we know home ownership is a privilege; but it's tough to remember when a thin coat of white powdery film coats every thing in the house despite the plastic sheeting. We are tired of microwaved meals and using a makeshift sink of a spigot and hose outside. The interior noise makes driving around in the heat and traffic seem like peace and quiet.

Still I'm trying to keep my sense of humor about all this. Today's knee slapper: the workers say they should be through in another six weeks.

Summer 1988, *Cutting the Rug* *(I could have danced all night)*

It's not easy after 17 years of marriage coming up with birthday surprises for my husband. We're not one of those families that make a huge deal out of birthdays, still a little something is required. Since it was summer and the kids were at camp and most of our friends were out of town and we were sick of eating out from out kitchen remodel, I gave my partner an unforgettable surprise. I blindfolded him, shoved him in the door of a new dance studio and beamed, "Meet Maureen: she's going to teach you how to do the foxtrot!" Not since I pried my last child's fingers off my leg and left her at the first grade door have I seen such a facial expression.

I have to confess I've always had fantasies of being Ginger Rogers, yet I married a man who hates to dance. Part of the reason may be that he grew up in small town Mississippi where his church opposed it. Or it might be that I'm 14 inches shorter than he is so we are a bit awkward waltzing about. But I think it's a part of my entire generation.

My peer group watched our parents dance to the big band sound; older kids jitterbugged while we boomers never really made much body contact. We sort of swayed to the soul sound, boogalooed around each other or in certain cases writhed around on the floor if you count "the gator." Later under psychedelic strobe lights anything passed for dancing. Nobody dances much, and I feel robbed.

Upon my return I found my husband much improved. "Slow, slow, quick, quick" This foxtrotting was not so tough. "Maureen says that if I'm stepping on your toes than *you're* not following," he grinned. So I cut in and found that we dance pretty much as we live…imperfectly, with fun and humor, certain panache, occasionally stepping on each other's toes.

The following night, the studio was having an open big band dance night for its patrons to practice. I wasn't exactly shocked when my husband called at 5 o'clock, "Honey…um…I forgot I have a dinner meeting."

I'm not worried. We have an anniversary coming up.

The next year I surprised him with a scuba instructor in the neighbor's backyard pool. This he liked and off to dive in Mexico we went.

Winter 1988, *Brace Yourself (Bonding with the rebels)*

We're into braces at our house. Not since the birth of my babies when all around me felt compelled to reminisce about labor and delivery have I heard so many war stories. Most of my fellow parents are moaning about the high cost of American's obsession with orthodontically perfect teeth. I'm not complaining. When my firstborn announced he hated math and that PE was his favorite subject, while crooked Bugs Bunny teeth began supplanting his pearly whites, and my husband started grousing about the point of building college trust funds, I wasn't worried.

My gut reaction was that the best thing we could do for our kids was get them a good set of braces. I was not merely heralding the Baby Boomers' rush toward plastic. Wise mother that I am, I knew instinctively that it was not so much one's early math scores in budding adolescence as a sense of connectedness with peers that helps produce well adjusted kids. And nothing promotes peer bonding so much as a mouth mold. Braces are the early adolescent silver badge of honor, which precedes membership into the heavy metal club of teenage—driving a car.

The parents' jitters over the ortho's bills is actually that nagging subconscious knowledge that this is the beginning of adolescence, which will not end until one's child cancels out one's presidential choice with his ballot at the polls. Meanwhile my 13-year-old takes pains imaginatively to describe the process to his amazed siblings while writhing and gagging. He details the goo, that nasty tasting stuff, and the agony when the appliance tightening begins.

When I paused from sorting through the bills and inserted that I had had five years of braces, retainers, and headgear so I remembered it well, wide-eyed they asked how that was. "Oh not bad. Just a couple of hours of unbearable pain."

Silence. Respect. The generation gap has been breached. Pity the parents of kids with perfect teeth.

April 14th 1988, *Spring, Soccer and Ice Cream (Sugar and Spice)*

Nothing ushers in spring quite like the parents and kids in the parks huddling up for soccer. Nothing makes me smile more than watching very young children galloping after that black and white ball while a young parent/coach tries to impose some sort of order on the melee. My second grade daughter has belatedly begun her soccer career, and after having watched what seem like thousands of games that her brothers played, I am struck by the difference. Phil Donahue will scream but little girls and boys are as different as vanilla and chocolate ice cream, and I say *vive la difference*. Who wants swirl?

The initial attempts at any childhood endeavor are not to be missed. The first ballet recital where the swans go in different directions, the first football season when the pads and helmets are more important than the game, the first band concert which sounds like a Salvation Army ensemble... the first soccer season. Surveying the little boys is like watching a litter of puppies tussling on the ground. Occasionally one will just stop and stare up at a passing jet. Little girls, on the other hand, cluster together giggling, adjusting each other's hair bows, admiring dangle rings, and when a latecomer arrives they all run over squealing en masse, "Micheeeelllle!" The earnest coach may be left giving a pep talk to the grass.

The burning issue on my daughter's team is whether to change the name from the Blue Scots to the Bluebonnets, or the Blue Ribbons. For boys it would have been the Blue Meanies or the Blue Busters. Nevertheless, by the second season there is a shift. It doesn't take long, for the competition is keen, the synchronization is slick, and the act is polished. All too soon the kids become veterans, and style melts away for substance.

Then when the referee blows the whistle and the games begin, there is no distinguishing between chocolate and vanilla. It's all just ice cream.

May 1988, *Motherhood Revisited (No more womb at the inn)*

Around forty, women purportedly go through a little passage in life when they make one last stab at dramatic change. Those with careers may stop and have babies; those full-time mothers may undertake a career or consider having one last child as the nest begins to empty. Or so the gurus tell us. While I like to think of myself as something other than a statistical norm, lately, much to my surprise, I have found myself musing over the motherhood option. When I mentioned this to my husband he stared at me and responded, "What? Are you nuts!"

I decided to test the waters by keeping our four-month-old goddaughter for a weekend. I'm cured. The high tech baby gear alone was too much. The stroller could do tricks. The old playpens of yesteryear have given way to "easy to assemble" pack n' plays. I suppose I'm the last of a vanishing breed–a mother who knows how to fold cloth diapers two different ways depending on gender.

I spent a lot of time wiping…runny nose, drooling chin, sticky fingers, and muddy bottom. The paradox of the sheer drudgery and sheer absorption that is the job of caring for the very young is a profound mystery, one that is not to be missed.

I could not keep my hands off this angel. Baby's skin is to be touched, nuzzled, kissed, their forms to be cuddled and rocked. And what silly things we do to make a baby smile! There is no magic age for childbearing, no correct number for family size, only a finite amount of physical stamina. After only two nights of midnight and 4 a.m. feedings, I realized, nostalgically, my time has passed.

Memories of frantic searches by flashlight in the yard one night for a favorite dropped pacifier resurfaced. Images of trying to force drops of sticky pink medicine down gagging little throats came floating up. Those long repressed memories in my salad days of trying to cook dinner with a crying four-month-old on one shoulder and a wailing 20-month-old attached to my leg came surging forth.

How do parents manage? Somehow when it's your time you just do. Last weekend with our baby goddaughter, we ordered out for pizza.

Summer 1988, *Moving On* (*When a buddy gets transferred, hard on kids*)

"Mom, Jack's moving," my crestfallen oldest son

confided. It's summer, a time when among other things people move—houses, cities, sometimes even countries. This I know, for I was a child of the international corporate move. So when my beleaguered oldest came home with the news that his best friend in the neighborhood was moving, I stopped what I was doing and commiserated. "That's tough. You're going to miss him a lot. I am so sorry."

And I was. I liked Jack, and his family too. This kid went all the way back in my young teen's life to kindergarten soccer. They'd been in carpools together, grew up playing army, helped build The Fort in our garage, and been in the debacle of the homemade bomb from a chemistry set. He was excited when we got our puppy and worried about my son's broken arm. In the last seven years, they'd gone from short pants, braces, laser tag and remote-control cars to their first rock concert. They had started pumping iron to impress…girls.

Was the lump in my throat for his loss or the images of my own childhood: three different sixth grades, a different seventh, and a different eighth? Yet with a move there is the initial wonder of change. Fresh faces can be invigorating. Life becomes a clean page where nobody knows you wet your pants the first day of first grade or that you had acne at thirteen. But also nobody remembers you were the lead in a school play or who your grandparents were.

Is there anything lonelier than trying to decide where a safe table to plant your tray in a new lunchroom is? It's hoping, hoping your new shoes, the ones your mom made you buy, will be cool at your new school. It's hanging around nervously, tentatively waiting for someone to approach and strike up a conversation who has not been assigned to do so. For a mother, it's not knowing where the hardware store is, where to get a haircut, having no one to wave to while driving around unfamiliar streets. For parents to instigate a move, it's trying desperately to make it all worthwhile.

Moving is realizing just how replaceable we are. The reality sets in before the first box is ever packed. It's when a mother calls to inquire about your housekeeper or babysitters or to see if she can get your carpool spot. For a smaller child, it's no longer being included in birthday parties because your mother won't be around to reciprocate. For a teenager, it's dropping out of spring practice because you won't be on the team next year. Moving is not having enough time for the whirlwind of packing up and saying goodbye, and then having too much time with no friends once you've arrived in unfamiliar surroundings.

For those left behind, it's just missing being able to drop by and visit or play depending upon the age. Just as wet sand quickly fills in our footsteps as we walk down the beach, life seeps in to fill up the void left by the boxes. Sort of. "We'll just have him come visit, and I bet you can go there too." I tried to console my son. We both sighed, knowing it would never be the same.

And guiltily I wondered if I could get Jack's mother's carpool day next year.

Fall 1988, *Life with Teenage Clones (The embarrassment of having a mother)*

There's a crowd at our house. It's not only that our kids are getting physically bigger and our house, even with a recent addition, feels like it is shrinking. It's that it's now filled with so many people. I'm not talking about friends and neighbors whom we welcome and enjoy. I'm referring to the mob that has moved in since both my sons entered junior high, namely "everybody" and "they."

"Everybody" is a lot of people although "they" can never be specifically identified. For example, a request to tie shoelaces is met with a forceful rebuttal that "everybody" wears their shoes that way. "You mean 650 kids at middle school are walking around with untied laces, and there are not several sets of stitches daily caused from people tripping over each other's shoes?" I deflect. This sort of verbal parry and thrust goes on constantly. I try to refrain from saying the "because I said so" of my own childhood.

Everybody can talk on the phone whenever they want. Everybody gets more allowance than my kids. Everybody has better bikes, cooler clothes, and more stuff than my boys. It is a source of endless consternation to my budding teens that my husband and I are not more attuned, more sensitive to what everybody thinks of us. Our indifference strikes them as the height of sheer folly.

Sometimes my sons feel compelled to slump down in the back seat, rolling heavily-lidded eyes heavenward, letting their jaws hang slack, to indicate to everyone non-association with the family group when driving as a unit. According to my boys practically the whole world, in fact, "they" are watching us eating, dressing, talking, walking, or living in some way that might jeopardize our acceptability. I suppose the Kennedys have long endured this sort of scrutiny, but our celebrity status is a recent phenomenon that dovetails neatly with our kids' entry into adolescence. I think it is evanescent and will last only a few years, probably until my sons go to college.

Then, as I recall, a desire for individuality and uniqueness from "they" surfaces. How do I know this? "Everybody" knows this.

Holidays 1988, *Family Visits (Love the in-laws... still)*

My husband walked in the door, tugging at his tie with the weary look that said, "What am I doing with an enormous mortgage fighting city traffic instead of being a photojournalist backpacking in Nepal?" I get those feelings too.

"Your mother called." I informed him while preparing a rather large meal. His response was a guarded but neutral, "Oh?"

"They've decided to come a day early, which means they are en route right now. It seems your Dad's doctor's appointment was cancelled so, how did she put it...'They believed they'd just come on and come rather than drive halfway.'" I went on to tell him I cancelled our dinner plans with friends, had skipped my board meeting to clean up the house, that we were having lasagna and..."

"Well, why didn't you just tell them to wait until tomorrow?" was his exasperated response. Yeah right.

"Never mind, I want them to come, it's just that I'm behind now and…"

This was followed by an exchange of shoulda, couldas that was only interrupted by the blare of the new electric guitar we had somehow been conned into letting into our house. He departed upstairs to quell the teenage racket while I was left to my own thoughts about how just as grandparents retire and children become teenagers our generation is facing mid-life crisis.

As he descended shaking his head, we both just burst out laughing at life its ownself. Just then the doorbell rang. We took a deep knowing breath and walked arm in arm to open the door shooing the barking dog out of the way.

"Hiiiii! COME IN!" we gushed in unison.

February 1989, *Treasure* (Nothing better than age 8)

I was about to tell my daughter on the last day of her life as an eight year old, for it was her birthday eve, that she needed to pick up her room before friends trooped over for her festivities. I was able to catch myself before issuing cleanup orders and observe this, my baby, deeply absorbed in arranging her treasures on the rug in her room. Unseen, I was able to study what, to the casual observer, might have been a random strewing of junk, some adults might have even said "a mess." Out of the chintz box in which she stores her *objets d'art* she had selected:

•a pink oval box decorated with rosebuds, a remnant from some soap I had once received

•multi colored plastic paper clips arranged like the petals of a daisy in the lid of a candy tin

•several strips of purple chiffon fringed with silver cut from an old Barbie dress arranged just so

•some plastic pink balls filled with liquid which can be chilled to use as "permanent" ice cubes in beverages

•tiny bows leftover from Christmas ribbons

•a few chandelier prisms so that they caught the light from her window

•a couple of diminutive china plates from a long ago tea set

•an acrylic star which looks as if it may once have held candy

•an old fashioned cut glass doorknob which has fallen off one of the doors in our house which anchors her design

And the chintz box harbors innumerable other objects she has not selected for this particular project.

I love these artfully arranged treasures as much

as she does. In the mind of a one-last-day-eight-year-old they are precisely placed. Her assemblage is as carefully crafted as a Louise Nevelson box or an Alexander Calder mobile. That it is composed of found junk still makes it art and not kitsch....at least to my daughter and her mother.

Things that are pretty, sparkly, and tiny just dazzle this child. How can I bottle this? In her world of True/False, fill in the blank, give the best possible answer, how can I keep her vision her own, how do I guard against standardization? What if, heaven forbid, she begins to see the world through the eyes of people who sit around publishing houses producing those less than fascinating textbooks?

She is startled by my growl, "Would you just stop growing up! Stop it right now!"

Reading my mock angry expression she throws back her head and laughs. "No way, Mommy."

Spring 1990, *Columnist takes first in state!*

Columnist Len Bourland was judged *Best in State* this week by the Texas Press Association. Her column, "At Our House," appears bi-monthly. "A wonderful column about a little girl's treasures and the mother who pauses to recognize the real treasure of that moment–Len Bourland is a treasure–both as mom and writer" wrote the Kentucky Press Association judges who selected her columns tops in the state.

March 1989, *PES (Not to be confused with PMS, also at our house)*

Tonight for dinner we're having one artichoke, two sweet potatoes, some rice, peas, sliced apple, rolls, chicken (as in chicken again), lima beans for a family of five. As I surveyed the plates I could detect no brown spots or any stringy things on the deboned chicken, and I made sure none of the peas or limas were touching the rice. The sweet potatoes and artichoke were for the parentals. One child had milk, one water, and one juice. You see, my children suffer from PES...picky eater syndrome. This has been around since birth when my sons began to spit out baby food. My firstborn had multiple allergies, and his brother just learned to be picky at the feet of a master. My daughter has had a funny stomach since birth, when I used to weigh her weekly on the vegetable scales at the Jitney Jungle on Fortification Street in Jackson, Mississippi.

I have the only son in America who does not like ground beef. He wails that I'm serving cat food if meat loaf appears. This kid won't eat a hamburger, tacos, and spaghetti. Hot dogs he likes. The brown thin kind, not the fat red ones. He prefers anything artificial to the real thing, Tang to orange juice, margarine to butter, Cool Whip to whipped cream, instant oatmeal (with maple and brown sugar) to stovetop stirred. As a preschooler he used to fixate on one food and eat nothing else for months. When he told me at age five the "peanut butter part of his brain died" I panicked until we found bacon. When he gagged once on applesauce, I managed to convince him it would go down with cinnamon. My pediatrician said not to worry, he was healthy, not to make a big deal out or food or have control issues. His kindergarten teacher told me not to bother sending the same box of raisins every day.

"Don't worry, there's one kid who daily brings exactly three wheat thins and a slice of white bread," she shrugged.

I occasionally try to serve something new. The miracle of the fishes and loaves occurs every time I serve fish as there is actually more fish on the plate after the meal than when I serve it…or so it seems.

We are the car that has to pull out of the drive in window line at McDonald's after ordering so that the plain chicken sandwich can be brought out to our car…

just meat and bread which is then carefully sniffed for no hint of mayonnaise by my PE. At his first five-day camping experience this child stayed alive by sucking down tubes of toothpaste he bought at the camp store, we later learned.

I don't take this personally. And one year a football player/hero counselor got my son to try a burger or else he "would smash his face." He chomped. As long as it was not mom issuing ultimatums like that, I was fine with that approach. I was determined never to repeat that ghastly experience of watching my brother being force-fed uneaten chop suey for breakfast the next morning by my Depression era father, and then throw up. Besides, I myself gagged on spinach, avocados, tomatoes, anything lumpy or scratchy like squash as a kid. My siblings and I all wanted to sit by the drawer at the breakfast room table so we could stealthily dump food.

As they got older, peer group pressure got to my kids anyway. They now all eat pizza (pepperoni only). Or maybe they like the fact that the Domino's guy at the door means parents are going out. Now I just try to serve something I like and have at least one thing each child will eat on the table. There are always leftovers. Would I get a better result if I just box them up, put them in a white sack and have it delivered to the front door?

Spring 1989, *New Math (Too much for old minds)*

"Get off the phone and do your homework," I flatly intoned to my ninth grade son.

He protested he needed help with his algebra, and he was doing his homework. Homework consults, right. I assured him his father and I could help. It seemed the impasse involved a mixture (in grams) of various nuts. Groceries. My expertise. I could do this.

Omigod. It was a word problem. I hated those. Hmmm. Let's see, the peanuts would be x, the cashews y so z would be...My son interrupted. We were not to have three unknowns, only two. Ok. I reread the problem slowly. I could see the answer but only by doing it backwards. No, no, was the protest. He had to show his proof. Hmm. I called over to my husband the doctor, who was cowering behind a newspaper. We were attracted to each other in college by our mutual loathing of calculus. He studied the problem. He came up with a ratio of peanuts to cashews that would yield a 100% solution of mixed nuts. My son was getting flushed. They could not do ratios; this was specifically to show the proof of an algebraic equation.

We finally let him call back his friend while I,

now frazzled, debated what to do. A Jacuzzi, a glass of wine, some Mozart? I did not want visions of SAT tests in my head before bed. Actually I could hear the fractured strains of Mozart as my daughter finished practicing her piano. She then strode in and demanded three friends for a spend the night party this weekend.

"Nope, your brothers are each having company and that would be eight kids. Too many. You can have one."

See? I can still do math when I have to.

Still spring 1989, *Piano Recital Best When Over*
(Perform, dammit)

We can finally kick back and enjoy the summer. My nine-year-old daughter has just had her first piano recital. My husband and I cleared our calendars for this momentous occasion, because our sons had been piano dropouts and never gotten that far. My sons went on to drums and electric guitars but that is garage recitals with buddies not involving us.

Judging from my child's reluctance to practice, (and frankly, an ordinary ability) this might well have been our only recital.

Remembering our own recitals, we had a case

of the jitters. My mother-in-law confided once she had to give her son a Valium to get him onstage. When he and his brother left the piano keys so sticky from their bubble gum hands after one duet, they were not invited back. I enjoyed piano until I discovered boys, and that was the end of that. No jitters for this kiddo. She has, like her peers, been filmed since birth at myriad activities and watched her own video performances from sports and plays on our TV. Unconcerned, she spent the day, not practicing, but cutting out faces of her favorite Dallas Cowboy cheerleaders to decide on who was the prettiest. (She and her father favored "Sherry.")

Why are we inflicting piano lessons on a little gal who clearly is no musical prodigy? Is it so one day she can sit down and plunk out "Jingle Bells" at Christmas? Or are piano lessons, like vitamin pills, just "good for you" while growing up? I marvel at those mothers who can get their kids through many years of practice so that they can pick out a tune well into adulthood.

It is certainly a testimony to parental doggedness to listen to a roomful of kids at varying ages play many of those same recital pieces of my own youth. The audience smiled a collective smile as a kindergartener tapped out "Skip to My Lou" and was enthralled with the high school senior's accomplished Chopin. My own child's mini Mozart was flawless, if a bit mechanical. Upon reflection about piano recitals, I think it isn't the performance of the piece or the level of expertise that is important, but the sense of accomplishment a parent can offer the child. Or is it vice versa?

May 1989, *Student Driver (An adrenalin rush for all in the front seat)*

I don't know if it's that I'm coming up on 40, or that this is the last year of the 80s, but my life has hit a milestone of sorts. Actually, my firstborn just got his driving permit. I've been trying to steel myself for this for some time; I bought the closest thing to a tank I could find, a Suburban, and have been practicing meditation and relaxation techniques. When out in the country on back roads, I've been giving both my boys a spin at the wheel. Still, there is some sort of cosmic joke that at the exact point at which communication with a teen is at its lowest, the states decree you can sit in a vehicle in a city with horrendous traffic and "teach" your kid to drive. To add further stress to the psyche, you realize given the sweet, happy nature of society today that every time your student driver gets behind the wheel your entire net worth is on the line. Not a soothing way to begin or end the day.

Last week we've hit one tree (slightly) and lost a hubcap to the curb that got too close to the car on a park job. I called the insurance company to check on how much our rates would escalate. "Lady don't ask, a fortune," the agent informed me...if he is in an actual fender bender. That's the good news. Next year my other son gets his permit. It seems Texas has some of the highest rates around.

My son used to get "itchy toes" just a couple of years ago when riding shotgun with me around town, (he'd bend down and mutter his foot itched every time we passed a car that might have some girl in it that would recognize him with the most embarrassing person a young teen can be seen with, his mother). Now he wants me in that car riding shotgun whenever possible so he can drive. My husband tells me to relax when I tell him my jaw stays clenched from mashing on an imaginary brake as I clutch the dashboard on our little excursions around town.

So I sent them both to the grocery to pick up a forgotten item the other evening. My spouse returned looking chalky.

"Do you have any idea how narrow the lanes are on Northwest Highway!" he sputtered.

Aaah, he'd had that wonderful feeling of nearly crashing into every tree and stop sign flying by the passenger window with the new driver's fear of the centerline. I just smiled. Going to the grocery store. The thrill is back.

Summer 1989, *Summer Camp (Survival of the fittest)*

I've spent all week getting three kids ready for summer camp, which amazes my husband who can't figure out what would take so long. Try motivating early teens into ironing on nametags, folding and layering the stacks of underwear, shorts, bathing suits, towels, and sheets not to mention inserting a rain poncho, postcards and everything else deemed essential by the checklist.

"Mom it never rains, nobody will want my clothes, I never send them to the laundry, I won't change my sheets, and I won't write unless they make me. I'm outta here."

His brother was right on his tail. Their idea of packing was just to wad some of the stuff up and shut the trunk. I just redid it, although probably only the top layer will ever be used, and everything else will come home with that dank, mildew odor that only summer camp can impart. Probably their mess should have stayed, but I just had to try to send them off right.

My daughter on the other hand was busy hand decorating her trunk and packing all of her favorite outfits. She was horrified I would send her with old frayed towels, which is what I save them for. I tried to explain that camp laundries specialize in turning clothes into cardboard, and she just needed her old stuff on this her first year at her brothers' camp. She insisted on a pink laundry bag and had made a list of her 14 best friends to write during rest time. She needed new ponytail holders, several brands of shampoo, and an extra pair of sheets just in case hers got gritty. She's nine.

I was both relieved and nostalgic after getting them on the bus. I went off to get ready for a much anticipated grown up getaway. Then to combat Mommy withdrawal, I decided finally to clean out the kids' rooms. I promptly flushed the goldfish down the toilet, as I had no intention of cleaning that bowl out and would just go buy another one right before camp pickup. My daughter's nest of little notes and girly things gave me an inward smile. When I got to the boys' room, I discovered wadded up detention slips, contraband girlie magazines, cherry bombs and Skoal. That was the limit. I fired off their first letter from home.

"Dear guys. Just cleaned out your room. Be glad you're in Missouri. Mom"

August 1989, ***Two for the Road*** *(Felt like the marriage was working)*

I'm sorting through the mail. A big stack accumulated while my husband and I took a blissful vacation together while all the kids are at camp. After two weeks of being alone, we're reminded of what being married really is. It's his using your toothbrush when he can't find his; it's eating together at restaurants and still having lots to talk about that doesn't involve kids. It's going shopping together, even if just for groceries. It's teamwork at the airport. It's living out of one suitcase. It's coming home to the mail, which is a microcosm of our lives.

There is, above all, junk mail. Lots of it. Some is cleverly disguised as urgent telegrams or dated documents, but junk nonetheless. We quickly toss that aside and make a stack of the largest category, bills. It doesn't even matter if we mistakenly throw one out, because as surely as whiskers sprout forth after shaving, a bill will always resurface. Occasionally, we find a treasure in the paper blitz, a personal note or invitation that we put aside. Then we find it; we hit gold. Letters from our kids at camp, the ones their counselors made them write to get Sunday fried chicken. We smile. We savor the two or three predictable lines from each child.

We're home.

January 1990, *A Hair-raising Experience (A great hair day is a great day)*

All my just turned ten-year-old daughter wanted for her birthday was a permanent, which left me weepy. Tears streamed down my face as I inhaled the familiar ammonia fumes of the perm we'd selected for her hard to wave locks. My hairdresser flatly refused to put chemicals on her baby fine wisps. It was not without trepidation that I sectioned off and wound tissue paper to her ends then onto little plastic rollers. Neither of us wanted her to be bald for her upcoming party. I think my misting eyes were also for the realization that she is dangerously close to putting away her childish ways of pigtails and braids and hair bows to enter into that perilous state called womanhood.

Women spend a lifetime between the yin and yang of being feminine and feminist. She wants to do anything her brothers do, but she also wants to look pretty. While men can be vain about their locks, most women just have more of the stuff and spend a lifetime cutting, coloring, straightening or curling, highlighting, moussing and styling their hair. I've never known a female who was satisfied with her hair for very long. Having a bad hair day really is a big lady thing.

I hated home permanents growing up and was one of those collegians who rolled her very long hair on orange juice cans to make it hang straight as a board. It is a mystery to me why a wad of fuzz is considered stylish. Today looking like a cross between Louis XIV and Art Garfunkle is all the rage: going "natural." Trying to pick through a freshly washed perm is like combing out a wet, matted poodle...anything but natural. But this is what my daughter wants; in fact it's all she wants, so I oblige. We can always cut it off if it's a disaster.

I must not have rinsed out all of the neutralizer because she reeks. The chemical odor announces her presence long before she enters a room. Her brothers' teasing is merciless. She is unperturbed and feels exquisitely grown-up and fashionable. At least for today her cowlicks do not grieve her. She loves her hair.

Spring 1990, *Grand Slam* (*Ann Landers doesn't understand the young male gods*)

I just read in Ann Landers that you should never yell or slam doors unless the house is on fire. Well then, our house is literally ablaze with emotion. Our front door takes a daily pounding that can only be described as "punishing." I defy Ann Landers to tell American male teenagers to talk in anything other than a roar. (They can't help it. They're all partially deaf from years of blaring rock music. Heavy metal is not the do-wap or soul sound of yesteryear.)

There's a screw missing on our front door handle which can't be replaced because all of the threads have been stripped out–no doubt from years of being wrenched by kids who like to wham the front door and make the glass rattle on the way out.

No doubt Miss Annie associates slamming and yelling with anger, but there are many reasons for an adolescent, especially the male of the species, to slam doors. Yes there's the furious slam after a muttering child has been sent to his room for some offense. But it is also a punctuation mark for excitement.

"Mom, my ride's here…bye." Wham.

Or the anxiety during exams while tearing

downstairs "I'm gonna be late!" Wham.

It doesn't matter whether it's a car door, a refrigerator door, or a front door, for a male teenager these are pressure release valves for raging hormones, vehicles to express machismo. The rule of thumb is the larger and heavier the door the more forcefully it must be shut.

The closed door seductively taunts a male teen, "How much can you bench-press?" SLAM the young gods answer. The trembling windowpanes giggle admiringly.

There is a single exception to this rule of slam. Male teenagers can gently, noiselessly, caressingly close even warped front doors...after curfew.

May 1990, *The Field Trip* (*The kid's right, the Hapsburgs really are ugly*)

It's field trip time and I have a vehicle with seven seat belts, which makes me a popular driver. As an art lover, I didn't want to miss taking the fourth graders to this museum. To the annoyance of my daughter I began a little background lecture on the masters, but when I whipped out an article on how a Japanese businessman had paid $82 million dollars for one of the artists they were going to see, I had their attention. They were pretty sure their own work must be worth at least a million when

64

they saw the Picasso.

Snickering past the nude statuary in the courtyard, the young appreciators of art were whisked away by a docent who asked them to describe what they thought a Picasso cubist painting was. Camouflage airplane hangar was one answer; another thought it was one of those pictures that must have hidden objects like a candlestick or a shoe. We were then marched into the Old Masters where an enterprising sleuth had wandered off course and spied a blasé bare breasted Madonna spewing an unlikely arc of milk into a baby's mouth "sort of like a squirt-gun." We were shepherded quickly over to the Velasquez room to study the Spanish Hapsburg portraits. The earnest docent in an attempt to make a point about brushwork asked what somebody could tell her about a king's portrait. A perky young man cut to the heart of the matter.

"He's really ugly."

Aaah, the weak Hapsburg chin. Trooping back outside the ever-observant young man pointed out a distant painting of Saint Bartholomew being flayed alive to a gaggle of horrified girls.

On the way back to school, I was trying to reinforce some of the docent's points when pandemonium broke out in the back. One child was screaming hysterically that her seatmate's wart had fallen off and landed on her. I put on a Rod Stewart tape.

I'm afraid that all my seven passengers will remember about that museum trip where they saw their first Picasso was that Mrs. Bourland played Rod Stewart music and Amy's wart fell off. Did they absorb anything about masters of Spanish art? I have no idea. Sometimes you just have to expose kids to art…warts and all.

Fall 1990, *Middle East Hits Home (Desert Storm and boy-men hormonal storms)*

It would not take much to induce my two high school sons to cease studying for their midterms last week. Certainly a war, Desert Storm, was grounds to discharge biology and geometry notes to sit glued to the TV…the idiot box has just been transformed into a shrine of information. Not since JFK's assassination do I recall being so addicted to news– news, which both repels and attracts yet is difficult to absorb in its enormity and significance.

My sons' patriotic fervor and enthusiasm fill me with bemused pride…and gnawing anxiety. They have feasted on a steady diet of Rambo and Schwarzenegger movies since early childhood. When I last returned from the grocery, a small army of male teens was watching the video of Top Gun reliving the thrill of aerial combat during a break from the real thing. They see a simple uncomplicated need to "take-out" bad guys. When George Bush talked about "kicking ass" he was talking the language of my 15 and 16 year-old, fast driving, stereo blaring, soon-to-be-soldiering age sons. Even my middle-aged husband wishes aloud he could take off and man a MASH unit in a combat zone. Are hormones related to this? I find myself seeking to calm my fears through routine: cooking, folding clothes, nursing a child with the flu. Yet like a moth to the flame I am drawn back to the flickering screen.

I have yo-yoing emotions. As a member of the 60s anti-war generation it is almost reflexive to say "Peace" and hold up two fingers. On the other hand, as a student and teacher of history I see few parallels to Vietnam politically or strategically. Yet every soldier is someone's son. On the other hand, you teach your children early on to face down the playground bully.

In my Rolodex of emotions I think the one I share most with my family is pride in my country. Even the cultured set at the Dallas Symphony belted out with gusto the national anthem the other night. My pride is tinged with sadness when I realize it takes a crisis to make us realize the fragility of freedom and how connected we are as Americans. Even my fifth grader marched in and announced, "We must all support our troops." From the mouths of babes.

Winter 1991, *A Little Modesty, Please (Lounge lizards of the weight room)*

In the cholesterol free, oat bran, naturally Lite, health crazed 90s I have an answer to that oft-posed question, "Where have all the lounge lizards gone?" They've gone to gyms, fitness clubs, and Nautilus rooms everyone. I suppose if I were 21 instead of twice that age, if I looked great in purple spandex with color coordinated sweatbands and socks, I wouldn't care. But at my age I rank the ubiquitous guys in neon shorts and body shirts baring midriffs, who are draped over exercycles winking and greeting every gal who walks in the gym door, right down there with telemarketers and many politicians. It's hard enough to stretch and pound cellulite with all those nubile young females who are arrive in tie-dyed leotards, makeup in place, ponytails bobbing without having to watch some guy leer in the mirror and yell "AAAHHH!" as he lifts a barbell with a stack of weights. Then these peacocks dramatically towel off sweat while sauntering multiple times to the water cooler. Or there are those aging Don Juans who breathlessly sing along (loudly) with the intercom music while running nowhere fast on the treadmills.

My secret desire is to exercise with just my gender, preferably mostly my age group. I propose a time when those who want to exercise can do that and another time for all those who want to network, socialize, exhibit hot fashion wear with just about everything hanging out while working up a steam. My sons are constantly telling me to get with the 90s, but I'm not sure I want to. My puritanism doesn't just stop at the gym. Am I the only person who gets embarrassed watching douche and sanitary napkin commercials on television with my kids? Could we have a little modesty please?

The enlightened psycho-babblers are probably eagerly nodding their heads and clucking that this is a highly repressed woman or at the very least one resentful of aging, maybe missing a few hormones. Perhaps I'm not liberated and in tune. Maybe I should just put on a Walkman, don a leopard skin body suit, rip a T-shirt off one shoulder, go crazy and make a bunch of new friends at the gym.

On second thought, maybe I have enough friends.

Summer 1991, *The Boat That Won't Float* *(Males on speed)*

We bought a new boat. The neighbors must be speculating on why a family that has a five-year-old suburban with a slight dent in the rear and a seven year old Peugeot in the driveway made its newest transportation purchase a sleek, super charged ski-boat. It represents most of our discretionary income in the form of 36 hefty monthly installments. Maybe not a bad deal in June, but I have a feeling come January we might resent this macho water baby.

Let the record show that I voted for a used boat more in line with our other vehicles and budget, but I got outvoted. Three males ages 15, 17, and not a teen found this honey with an amazing sound system at the boat show last week. So lady are you bragging or complaining?

Let me clarify. The male minds rationalized that we needed a new boat lest we end up with boat trouble 90 miles outside of Dallas on an East Texas lake. This would be maintenance free providing more time for family fun. One weekend we packed for our inaugural boat launch, complete with skis and a picnic, and headed out. "Just turn the key and ski " was our new family motto. As soon as we were all aboard we did just that, except that the only sound was "thunk" not "vrrrroooom." Although we missed out on the sun as we headed home with our picnic, my husband was red nevertheless. We are spending next weekend meeting the dealer's mechanic at the lake.

Usually boats are named for females (I have no idea why). But my sons wanted to deviate from this norm with names like, Demon Studs, Honcho Sex Pistols, So Bad…things like that. My spouse did offer to name the boat after me to the horrified looks of my children. I declined the honor, but I did get to select the name.

Next weekend you can spot us on the lake, maybe even skiing, in…*Group Therapy*!

Fall 1991, *Cheerleading (From little girls to wannabe babes)*

My 11-year-old daughter has decided to organize a cheerleading squad for the sixth grade boys' football team for their local league games. Life has not been the same since. It seems she enlisted the support of a good friend to organize all the girls in the class ("to be fair") with her and her friend as co-captains. The reaction of her peer group has rocked her little soul. The phone has not stopped ringing. One or two thought it was a supremely dumb idea. A larger group immediately tried to take charge. Still others contemplated a rival squad. Mainly everyone showed up and fought. Tears fell and hormones rages. I stayed far, far away admonishing other moms to do the same. Some woman somewhere in Texas had shot another mother when her daughter didn't make cheerleader. A kindly gym teacher intervened. Should I be proud of her innovativeness or blunt this turn from academia? I am myself in a state of flux.

For this is my child who is a lover of books, a curious student with an inquiring mind. Will she soon stop competing with the boys in her class, instead demurring coquettishly as the experts tell us happens in junior high? Is this how it all begins as she assumes a support role to the dominant male jock? Can I look forward to her baking cookies for the boys who would never dream of reciprocating? Will an absorption in makeup, fashion, and hairstyle replace an interest in books and ideas?

And why does it bother me that each phone conversations begins with "I'm sorry, I'm not trying to be bossy or rude, it's just that since I thought of it…"

Her brothers would never talk that way. They would say something like, "Tough, man. If you don't like it you can kiss me where the sun doesn't shine and …"

Right now she's after me to teach her a few cheers, because she's seen my old photos with megaphone and pom poms cartwheeling for the Westminster Wildcats of my Atlanta teenage years.

"Mom what does two bits, six bits, even mean? It just doesn't make sense?" she queries.

Nothing about writhing around in a short skirt screaming and bouncing makes much sense. I do know that being a cheerleader beat being in the National Honor Society by a long shot. But Margaret Thatcher and Sandra Day O'Connor, who can see them as cheerleaders? I sense we are at a crossroads here. If I teach her cheers now, will she thank me years later when she hits the corporate glass ceiling?

My husband thinks I need to lighten up, that I'm wildly exaggerating by seeing this as a feminist issue instead of a normal phase in growing up. He assures me this will not lead to her becoming a bleached blonde babe dancing half naked before millions on TV instead of having a career path. "Besides," he snorted, "face your real fear. You're just worried you're on some mother's hit list."

September 1991, Family Portrait by Phil Stephens
***Park Cities People* as we are selected Family of the Week**

Expect the Unexpected. While this could stand as an axiom for any parent to rely on, it is a daily fact of life at this household. With everyone rushing off in different directions... the couple finds time to walk the dog together every evening, "sort of like a de-tox" he (*husband*) said. "I think one of the strengths of our family is that we all have a sense of humor about our family and ourselves." Len Bourland said. She wears many hats as columnist, radio commentator, instructor at the community college level, community volunteer, and of course, mom. They found the kind of values they wanted to instill in their family in the Park Cities. Len, in particular, could see her family sinking roots in a community, an experience she never had growing up as a self-described "child of the corporate move." They welcome friends and neighbors, keeping it loose and livable where the dog sleeps on the furniture and where they'll still be close in years to come.

December 1991, *The Media* (*It's all out there and everywhere*)

My husband and I were going on a business trip

to Boston. Since I had a son reading *The Scarlet Letter*, another one in American history, and a daughter in the throes of *Little Women*, I offered to bring back souvenirs. A photo of the House of Seven Gables, a postcard of the Old South Church, a picture of Louisa May Alcott's home? Nope. They all three ranging from 5th to 11th grade were interested in only one site, a photo of the Cheers bar, their favorite TV show. That's what Boston means to them. Again this year at Halloween I gave out candy not only to witches and ghosts but also to Bart Simpson, Madonna, and Hans and Franz. When I asked my lunch bunch whether they or the media had more influence on their kids, the gloom was palpable. My children, like their peers do not speak English. They talk in filmspeak, which is a mixture of jive talk, slang, and sound bytes from movies and *Saturday Night Live*.

I think my family is not atypical. When they were younger, it was fairly easy to limit shows and pontificate about the need for parents to monitor their TV sets. Lots of activities and bedtime stories would shield them from Hollywood values. Besides I had grown up with the *Mickey Mouse Club*, which segued, in later years to the *Twilight Zone* and those chilling Hitchcock thrillers like Psycho. That shocking line from *Gone With the Wind*,

"Frankly my dear, I don't give a damn" morphed into the pervasive expletives in practically every movie. Aren't kids in the 90s just doing what we did? And I rationalize that what they don't get at my house is pretty widely available just about anywhere.

The fact remains that there is very little shock value left in movies today. The violence, sado-masochistic sex, and explicit language are now routine. This is not only limited to R rated films. Watching the news with my daughter this past year I've had to explain rape, sexual harassment, bestiality, and pornography to my 11-year-old and am caught in the dilemma of wanting to educate her but also shield her from the seamier side of life.

I'm just grateful that what they seem to gravitate toward is humor. There's that. Cheers.

Winter 1992, *Lost and Found (More than the car going missing is going on here)*

I owe an apology to the car thieves of Dallas. Our old Suburban, the one I broadcast and put in print and to the police reported as stolen at DFW airport has been found...by me.

What exactly happened is this: We flew out of terminal 3E for a family post Christmas ski holiday.

I parked the car on level C in short term parking while everyone got out and took care of the bags. I wrote the level and place down on the parking ticket, that's how I know. Good old American after a flight delay flew us back late at night to a different terminal and gate. I took a tram back over to drive the car around while kids and hubby went to get the bags. After walking for what seemed like days, I could not find the car. In a panic I hailed a cab, went back to the other terminal and loaded up bags, super-annoyed family and had our non-English speaking, speed demon cabbie drive us back over to 3E to find our car. After a harrowing cab drive around and around every level with five people unable to spot our car, we decided it must have been towed and just went home. We were informed it had not been impounded; the license plate had not been recorded on camera leaving DFW so glumly I filed a police report. Dallas is the car theft capital of the world. Airport security said they would search all parking terminals.

The next several days were filled with paperwork, with insurance companies, police reports, renting a car, car shopping, undoing Christmas, laundry, writing holiday thank you notes, and life. The night after everyone finally went back to school, I sat bolt upright in bed at 2 a.m. after a vivid dream that my car was still at the airport exactly where I had parked it. I did not plagiarize this from the dream sequence from *Fiddler on the Roof*. I drove back my rental to DFW to level C short-term parking and there it sat forlornly.

My kids believe somebody took it joyriding. My astonished friends said, "Just say the police found it. No explanations. Nobody has to know the embarrassing truth."

This was also the exact reaction of my mortified family. Plus they reminded me it was my fault since I had parked the car. Never mind that they had all been in the cab looking, that the airport security had not been able to find it, and that we didn't subscribe to the Dick Nixon school of cover-ups and limited modified hangouts. Nor was I rationalizing that the cabbie just blew by one level or that our flight delay and the time and terminal change contributed. Nope it was my fault. There. A teachable moment.

I think this entire episode is not without value. I now realize why you can never find a parking place at the airport. There are probably hundreds of lost cars out there that have been abandoned by their owners for years. Finally, I'm going to pay more attention to my dreams.

The ticket for the car being in short term parking for two weeks was not free, neither was the car rental and a stiff cab ride. To recoup my losses I'm going to hangout my shingle...as automotive psychic.

And given nearly everybody's advice to stonewall, I also realize that lurking beneath the surface of even ordinary mundane lives must be incredible secrets.

Boy howdy, I didn't know what a prognostication that was.

SPIN

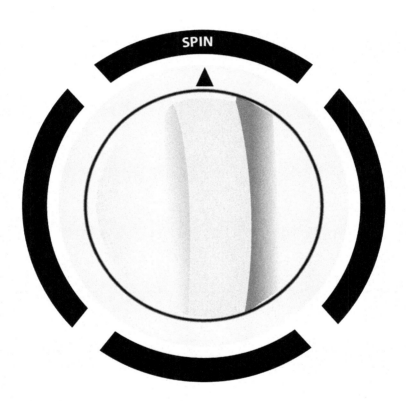

NORMAL'S JUST A CYCLE ON A WASHING MACHINE

Part Three: Spin Cycle at Our House

Life had just freed up for me after all the energy of raising children with a workaholic. Writing, broadcasting, teaching in my field of American history at a local junior college gave me a full calendar. Feminism had arrived after I had married right out of school, and I relished the new avenues opening up in the conservative South. Everything was great except for my husband's moodiness. So? We all have our foibles. Moods change just like Texas weather. You just wait them out or jolly somebody up.

Shortly after the car went missing, so did my spouse. Increasingly, he came home late, mumbled excuses about needing to get back to the hospital, but several times when I called there or his office to remind him of a child's event or something we had planned, nobody could find him. This was long before cell phones or caller ID. When he came home, it was with new wardrobe purchases and a new convertible; so why didn't I figure out he might be joining that great fraternity of mid-life guys who mess around?

Funny when the kids complained about dinner on the first day of school, I knew it wasn't about dinner; it was about the stress of a new year with lots of change. He became critical, of medicine, the kids, even the dog, and finally me. Instead of dropping back with perspective I began trying to fix things, as any adult child of alcoholics is prone to do. I had a soiree for our Congressman so doctors could complain about healthcare. I planned a family ski trip. I made sure there was no honey do list so coming home wouldn't be a burden.

Why didn't I suspect a dangerous liaison? Because I wouldn't have done it to him. Because he came from a rock solid Norman Rockwell church going tight knit family in small town Mississippi. Because we weren't fighting. Things were still ok in the boudoir. Wasn't I fabulous? I just trusted him. He had just bought me my first piece of nice jewelry at Christmas, and all our friends were laughing about husbands and wives going through menopause. Dave Barry had just written a screamingly funny book about it. (Before he got divorced.) Johnny Carson was doing his goodbye countdown on the "Tonight" show, and little did I realize watching in bed with my husband, we were doing our own countdown.

Then my moody, " best friend" got depressed. He began reading downbeat novelists and writing despairing, Byronic poetry, about feeling suicidal...until he confessed *he was having an affair and had fallen wildly in love. Unburdened of this secret his depression flipped into hypomania. Who was this guy?*

In a panic, I found the only person I knew whose husband had wigged out, and they had recently divorced. I dragged him to this therapist, who told me he was "a horse without a bit." Endlessly I self analyzed while trying to keep this from kids, family and friends Meanwhile, I was slinking into my closet curling up in the fetal position and just sobbing. I could not believe my own behavior. Why couldn't I get mad, or even? I was so distraught and nervous and losing so much weight the kids became alarmed, especially my sons. I would get everyone out of town to sports camps and...and... I would wait this thing out. My nest was under attack, and I would not let this happen. How could it be happening? We would move, or I would wait it out. Once the kids were gone I moved him out over the summer. I would awake at night from nightmares into a living nightmare. Three a.m. might find me cold and shaking in a hot shower despite the Texas August weather. My doctor had ordered me to drink milkshakes (that was a lifetime ago) to put on weight. All those country songs made sense. My heart literally hurt; it ached.

Then came my panic attacks. Surely if I read

everything I could find, I could figure this out. Self help books, Prozac, Xanax; my bedside table was getting a little crowded. Where had I failed? Was he ill? I just knew he loved the kids, and me, so how could he hurt us or leave us? After over 20 years of work and sacrifice, we had just completed a lake cabin, remodeling the house, and had careers blossoming. Our friends and kids were terrific. There were enough disasters in life with acts of God, disease, and war without creating calamity by blowing up a family. What was he thinking? When we were young, we had guffawed about doctors who did this. Despite my exhausting efforts word was seeping out. It was my oldest son's girlfriend who figured out nobody was home at night, when I took the kids to the beach. I feared for my boys on the cusp of manhood, but mostly for my pre-pubescent tweenage daughter. Their dad was their hero. This was surreal.

There is nothing quite as jarring as sneaking out to lunch and having women stop and stare, glance away and begin to whisper. I went to the grocery at night. I hid in dark movie theatres. I told a few out of towners first for support and advice. Friends got on airplanes or drove in and tried to intercede. Reluctantly, he moved back in, said half-heartedly he would break it off. Right before school started we rededicated our marriage vows with a few friends and the children, who were stiff with hurt and embarrassment. It had only been a summer. I would contain this thing. The misery index in our household that had only months before been a busy vibrant hub was palpable.

That marriage vaccination didn't take, and he was soon spotted about town in his convertible with his young babe. My brief hope was dashed. His mortified fundamentalist parents, who initially thought I had underappreciated their star, finally realized he was in total rebellion, and this was no dalliance. Ashamed they went underground. Would that he had gone to Woodstock in college, or gone to the military, or...well the stallion without a bit took off and never looked back. Nothing would ever be the same. All memories would forevermore be filtered through a new lens. The present was awful. The future had fallen down in mid flight.

Finally, I started interviewing divorce lawyers when this didn't blow over. I'd only slept with this one man in my life and now got tested for STD's. Humiliating. I wanted to stay in bed and die, but I needed to be both parents and two sets of grandparents for my kids. My sullen, sad, angry brood refused counseling but hunkered in with friends. It was nearly a year in limbo before I filed. I found myself in that great cliché or like the song says, I was "Going through Big D and I don't mean Dallas."

Despite my best efforts, the divorce was slowly progressing even as my oldest was graduating from high school. I wrote this lament for which ironically, I won an award before putting down my pen.

Press Release: *Park Cities People*

July 1993 Awards to Weekly Newspapers comes to the Park Cities again. The newspaper's second place went to the writing by Len Bourland, which drew the following comments: "Very good. Pure thought set down professionally. Very articulate."

May 1993, *Commencement*

There are few times in life, which are more seminal than graduating from school and going off to commence the process of learning where you want to direct your energies and how to pursue your dreams. It is a lifelong journey. There are few times when a mother's heart can be more laden with emotions than when her firstborn child graduates and leaves home. Which ones can I name? Joy, sadness, pride, hope. Of course your journey began on that other emotion laden day—was it really so long and so short a time ago—the one on which you demanded to be born? I pushed, the doctor pulled and there you were: an eight-pound miracle.

Reflection comes naturally. I rerun the mental video of your life in my mind frequently. Your christening, your first steps and words, your little green scooter bug, our love of the beach, your playgroups, the toy lawnmower you used to push behind your dad, your first coat and tie, your Cub scout years, your braces, camp closings, field days, school carnivals, carpools, cotillion, sex-ed, wrestling tournaments, your driver's license. But if you've learned nothing else your senior year, it is that life is ever-changing and not always filled with Kodak moments. There were also stitches, asthma attacks, car wrecks, tough teachers, tough breaks and enormous losses. If there is one emotion I do not feel at your graduation it is that of regret. There is not one argument or defeat or disappointment without purpose. There is not one more honor, or good grade, or victory that would have made your life any more than it is…a gift we, your family, had the privilege of sharing with you daily for a very short time.

Now that you've moved on, what gift can I give

you to sum up what you have meant? What advice, what dreams, and what wisdom can I impart? College is partying but it's cleaning up the next morning with a headache. College is all night cram sessions but it's learning how to share a bathroom and how to sort the dark clothes from the light. College is learning how to live in a community, but it's learning how to become a number as well. You'll have an abundance of nicknames, but you'll be your social security number, your student ID number, your selective service number, and your driver's license number. You won't get warnings or have coaches pressuring you to make good grades; you'll have to learn how to seek out help or flunk.

You'll learn about existentialism, LIFO/FIFO, and the ramifications of the Viet Nam War; but the most important lessons you learn will not be newly accumulated information; they'll be life lessons. It is important that you experiment, challenge, probe, and explore so that you can learn who you really are. It is an open-ended course of study. The most important task you have before you is to create a new sense of community, a family of friends and peers. For it is in your relationships with others that you will discover what is valuable in life. You will have the rare privilege of living with and sharing intimately in other people's lives.

You've already learned much from your own family...but you inherited us. Now you create your own world. One day you may want to choose a life partner. Choose wisely. You will form your own beliefs and value system. Think deeply. You will be in charge of your own physical well being. Stay well.

Never forget how many lives you touch, how valuable you are, and how much you are loved. And carry your home in your heart.

After a hiatus of over a year a new editor, the former editor of the Dallas Times Herald *called and asked why I had stopped writing? I asked him if he lived on the planet Xenon, that Our House was now just My House. Write about that he implored. I protested it was the Bubble. Nobody wanted to read about that. He told me it was time for the Bubble to break. A lot of unhappy readers reacted to my dirty linen on the front page of our suburban weekly, with this screaming headline:*

No doubt about it, Texas is hell on women, horses

There used to be a ride at the state fair called the Centrifuge...perhaps there still is. You would enter a darkened circular chamber, and as the ride began to spin around, your body would be slammed against a wall with no handholds. As if this wasn't enough of a dizzying, numbing sensation, while you were quelling nausea, the floor would suddenly collapse; the terror of having no ground beneath your feet as the momentum accelerated completed the ride. Then you were dumped unceremoniously into the sunlight to emerge dazed and blinking on wobbly legs. Divorce is like that.

It takes two years to serve a term in the House, three to go to law school, four to fight a world war, and somewhere in between to break down a marriage and family. To those of you who have missed my column, please know that having just emerged from my own ordeal, I have no desire to add to the O.J. Simpson, talk show confessional journalistic farce that pervades our country *ad nauseam*. I have borne witness to the best and worst sides of human nature, which, like a swirl yogurt, exist side by side in this community. And the stories bear telling.

There were days when I felt the pain of watching my nest under attack and my family being dismantled was more than I could endure. Always the gifts of flowers, a casserole, an encouraging note, or a friend would appear on my doorstep. As hellish days turned into gray months of legal limbo, I thought I could not tolerate the tackiness of my life. Inevitably people appeared with invitations, hugs, books, and jokes. And as the months turned to years, I wondered how I would physically manage on emotional empty to make the necessary transitions. Kindred spirits materialized to box up, move, unpack and celebrate new beginnings.

So my children and I have learned many life lessons as we struggle to walk unsteadily in our reconfigured lives. Having been submerged in my own soup these past years, it is with no small sense of wonder that I discover that the great gumbo of life is still roiling. I can appreciate it with a sense of hard earned wisdom, some perspective, even humor.

I have learned as a mother, one of the toughest things in life is to watch your children suffer, tougher and more necessary yet is to let them suffer. I have learned that there are miracles around us everyday if we open our heart to them. I have learned that the medieval divorce laws and court system in Texas are in drastic need of overhauling, and there is much truth to that old maxim that "Texas is hell on women and horses." I've learned how to close on a real estate deal, how to budget on Quicken, how to fix a toilet…over and over I have learned.

But the most important life lesson that my children and I have absorbed as we have become annealed through growth and change is that a family need not be dismantled. When a community responds, it can only be extended and nourished.

Just when I thought I was on emotional empty there was the next thing.

January 1994, *Bye Buddy (Even the dog dies)*

They say that over the years pets come to resemble their owners. That certainly seemed to be the case at our house. About ten years ago our neighbors had a litter of Bichon Frises. I then had nine and ten year old boys, and a four year old daughter. Having gotten past diapers and teaching all to tie their own shoes, the last thing I wanted was something else to take care of. But it was Christmas; my neighbors had a litter of puppies and this breed was not supposed to shed which would irritate my son's asthma. For all the world the pups looked like white fuzzy slippers. How though were we to make this pedigreed fou fou dog who would need grooming fit in with a family more suited to a mutt? Our Christmas "Snowball" looked too refined for us.

I only know that somehow he wormed his way into all of our hearts and each child's bed before very long and somehow took on the persona of a family composite. From my oldest tough son he learned bravura. Although frequently mistaken for a poodle, Snowball, aka "Balls" felt man enough for the female black lab down the street and guarded our house with the ferocity of a pit bull. From my little girl he learned sweetness and civility. He allowed himself to be patted raw at show and tell for years and to sit meekly on the sofa to have his tummy rubbed. From my middle son this dog became a social animal with a great sense of play. To watch this boy and his dog literally carrying on conversations was to behold two great personalities. Snowy grandly treed squirrels and learned to press down the electric car window to catch a breeze on his face at his brother's urging.

As my kids became noisy adolescents Snowball followed suit. He demanded walks, dragged his dish across the floor to be fed, and began to sneak out the back gate for neighborhood roams. He could never stay groomed, looked a little scruffy but adored life. Indeed he came to resemble our family.

We found Snowy dead on the curb a few weeks

ago on the last day of the year. There were no outward signs of injury, probably a glancing blow to the head or a stroke. My two college age sons wept openly as did my daughter who could not remember a day in her life with her dog. Our void is enormous, for in the last year our family has gone through the excruciating pain of divorce. I did not see how my children could bear more suffering, more loss, or how I could bear witness to their pain.

Yet the timeliness is becoming clearer to me. All my children had gathered for the holidays in our home that would soon have to go on the market that holiday morning. My middle son simply could not give up the body of his buddy to the vet for disposal. So holding the lifeless body in his lap we drove the 90 minutes to kind friends' country home. My sons dug ferociously into the winter packed earth a grave fit for a Great Dane. My daughter and I gathered stones for markers and branches with berries to place on top. Before we sealed the lambskin-lined box, we put in some pet treats, his bowl, and my son removed a cross from around his neck. Then we held hands, prayed and eulogized our friend. We knew we were burying a lot more than our family pet that day. We yet grieve, but there was some closure that has enabled us to pick up and move on.

And we are reconciled to the fragility of life.

Fortunately my sanity was somewhat restored when I was steered to a gifted psychiatrist. Having been through medical school with a husband, I knew the disdain in which they are often held by their own profession. This man was a godsend. Eventually, I was able to internalize what I had been assuring my children, "There is nothing you did or did not do that caused or could have prevented what this person did." Well mostly. I was more than willing to take some blame when I held out hope for marriage counseling; but by the time we got there, it was too late. Crazy time had already begun.

Summer 1994, *Depression (Way beyond bummed)*

"I don't know what we're going to do with her. Ever since she broke up with this boy all she does is cry."

My long distance friend's concern about her college daughter seemed more desperate than the usual mother's lament. Her daughter was experiencing more than a slump; her breakup was her first true love in a faraway cold Northeastern city that had her sobbing around the clock for the third straight month.

I asked if I might call her. This sensitive child

had been battling bulimia since her parents' divorce. I wondered aloud if she had difficulty getting out of bed, if she felt like going to class. It seemed she rarely left her apartment, even going to the grocery store seemed overwhelming. Did losing this relationship seem as scary as when her parents remarried and moved off? Affirmative. Did she feel like no place was home? At this point her sobs became nearly hysterical. Did she just want the pain to end?

"Yes."

I assured her I had felt that bad when my marriage ended, and she didn't have to feel that bad. Having been in a black hole I recognized a fellow sufferer of depression. A funny thing the mind. When we are in a state of happiness we know it won't last forever. But logic evaporates in depression, and the pain feels like forever. There is no hell like hopelessness.

That young lady is now on Paxil, an antidepressant, but her mother doesn't want anyone to know. Another friend from my high school days was weepy and flat. Her father was terminally ill while she was going through menopause. There was simply no joy in her life, and it was affecting her marriage. She knew she needed help when she escaped to her favorite beach but felt nothing.

The medical term is "anhedonia," a loss of pleasure over time. She now takes Zoloft, but she doesn't want anyone to find out. Yet another local friend's husband just turning 50 lost his job due to corporate downsizing while their teenager has a terrible attitude, and they fear she is using drugs. Increasing his jogging didn't help. He is now on Prozac but his medication is the family's big secret.

One reason Colin Powell chose not to run for the presidency was to spare his wife, who was once treated for depression, the cruelty of an ignorant, shaming public. Barbara Walters had it, so do 18 million Americans; yet depression is our dirty little secret in the land of opportunity. No doubt it's because in hushed tones we label it "mental illness," which conjures up crazy aunts in the attic, straitjackets, electro-shock treatments, and ax-murderers.

Stupid. The body is in physiologic distress and the synapses, which transmit the feel good endorphins to the brain, have shut down. Antidepressants allow them to function normally just as a bronchial dilator opens up airways for an asthmatic. Once mood is restored then you can work on coping. They don't work for everybody. The medication definitely doesn't make you happy, high, or make any problems go away. And depression is not a character flaw or weakness.

To those who snort we've become a nation of pill poppers, I can only retort, I hope so. When I have pneumonia I take an antibiotic, for a headache aspirin, antihistamines for hay fever. Why would I avoid a medical advance in depression? An internist, gynecologist, and psychiatrist all assured me my antidepressant was safer than aspirin when I took one during the divorce process.

To those naturalists who wish to go back to chewing on roots and stirring bark into tea, so be it. To the self-righteous who say buck up and get right with God, I would say may you never have your world shattered by the death of a child, rape, war, cancer or overwhelming grief or loss.

We are a society that worships at the altar of depressant drugs, namely booze, but can't even discuss the other side of that coin, anti-depressants, without getting extremely nervous. Now that's depressing.

The drugs may have changed, Lexapro, Effexor, and others have arrived, and Colin Powell segued into other famous depressed people; but I reran this article several times as requested over the years. People would still rather talk about their cancer or probiotics than antidepressants. Sad.

Being marginalized in the world of singledom began soon. To use the surgical analogy separation and divorce was like having a major vital organ removed without benefit of anesthesia. But then the little cuts just keep coming. The pharmacist who once called me Mrs. B., now handing me my antidepressants, using my first name while winking. The guy at the filling station who leaned into the window and was overly familiar. Getting seated at poor tables in restaurants when going out to eat with another single woman. Being culled from social events or when attending the waning invitations, feeling like I had to stay in the kitchen with the wait staff as women would come up to me if I talked to their husbands and protectively put their arms through theirs, as if I might move in. I was the last person who would go long on happiness by shorting another woman. I was beginning to see only the wives at lunch instead of mixed company.

The worst part of divorce is not downsizing or loss of lifestyle, although it is real and it hurts. (I hadn't enjoyed affluence for very long anyway.) It was trying with no energy to make a home in a lesser neighborhood, for a dispirited young lady going through puberty

"Why me!" she burst out angrily one day.

"Why not you? Or me. Neither of us is living in West Dallas or lost someone who was killed in a drive by shooting. This is the hand we were dealt so let's play it as gracefully as we can," was my response.

But while some people flee as if divorce is contagious, or rally for the initial phase, there are those who just stood fast. Lots of angels kept popping up.

September 1995, *"Uncle Kathy–Our Ms. Fixit" (First responders)*

Following pain or stress, the human psyche numbs out like an arm or leg with the blood flow cut off. The pins and needles that signify a return to feeling also signal the impending discomfort of renewed circulation. There are a few rare individuals whose talent is to accelerate the healing process. Some people retreat from the problems in other people's lives. Others teach the rest of us how to respond.

Living out of boxes, not knowing where the bathroom is in the middle of the night, computers and VCRs that won't plug into unfamiliar outlets, this is the reality of a move. If the move involves Dallas heat, downscaling after divorce, and depressed children, the effect can be overwhelming. Enter Kathy.

Affectionately known as "Uncle Kathy" for her good-humored avuncular advice and love of fixing things, she arrived at my house like a modern day Mary Poppins. From Mississippi she came with her toolbox, paints and shelf paper and went to work. She announced that it looked like we were camping out and needed to make our house a home, a place where we could choose to build only happy memories. She organized closets, hung pictures, towel bars, tie racks. She repaired a torn screen, painted a bathroom, and programmed the sprinkler. Room by room, drawer by drawer, she scrutinized space to make it more efficient, and ruthlessly she threw out what she deemed extraneous junk. The house began to have a humming noise, the sound of appliances churning and blowing.

Then she turned her eye to beauty, dubbing herself a budget minded Martha Stewart. "All five senses," was her mantra. She taught us how to dial the color back into the monochromatic affect after depression. So we replaced light bulbs with brighter wattage, trimmed shaggy trees for extra light. The smells of home cooked meals wafted throughout, and we tasted cookie dough, custard and cakes. We bought bath oils and new linens for touch. The sounds of *Enya* blared on the stereo and she had us belting out oldies but goodies. Plants, flowers, and bird feeders appeared.

Kathy insisted on life and growing things. Every room should be a safe haven, your home a refuge and retreat, was her motto. At the end of a week she surveyed her handiwork and pronounced the need to celebrate. So we whipped up a party and invited the neighbors in. Friends marveled at her energy.

"You should start a business," one said.

"But then it wouldn't be a gift," was her response.

She is no Pollyanna who has ice-skated over life's bumpy patches. This lady has coped with financial struggles, divorce and remarriage, a child on drugs, ailing parents, and one grandchild with Downs's syndrome and cancer. She is reconciled to the vicissitudes of life and has faced adversity with grace and practicality. She is a big believer in the power of community and spirituality.

But ask her what her talents are, she will laugh and shrug and respond, "I'm just a housewife."

The death of a family through divorce can be worse than an actual death. If a spouse dies the community is quick to respond. Not so with divorce. Today it is so acceptable that it is difficult to overlay the template of a generation ago. It still had a stigma, and the woman usually bore the brunt. Or as my attorney said, the husband gets custody of the money while the wife gets custody of the kids. If it is like the stages of death, I had gotten past denial, bargaining, depression and finally came that all empowering anger. At first, being in my own bubble, I didn't know anyone that had been through an affair. Then people crawled out of the woodwork and I wondered who had not. Work it out if you can, but take care of yourself was my advice to the suffering. Still I shuddered when I got these kinds of phone calls.

A reality check on Texas divorce laws (Hell hath no fury...)

The woman's voice was tremulous and small as she poured out her story on the phone. I was not acquainted with her yet I was all too well acquainted with her story. She was descending into hell, and I could offer her no solace knowing what I now know. I reached for the Maalox and thought I'd rather have a root canal than this conversation.

"I really cannot recommend any divorce lawyers," I sighed.

It's not that my opinion of attorneys is so low, it's that the laws under which they are constrained are so patently unfair. After a quarter of a century this displaced homemaker is not only still reeling over the demise of her marriage, but also worrying about how to finish raising her children alone, about approaching 50, or maintaining a decent job and economic survival. So I told her to get in her car, get on the freeway, cut in front of a Rolls Royce, slam on the brakes and get rear-ended. Then she might get the financial security she needed, but she would not get it in the antediluvian family code of the Great State of Texas.

Texas is a community property state based on the Old Spanish agrarian law when most people were farmers. If a man up and left his family the wife got half the farm with the children to work it. It was not only a division of assets but future income and financial security as well.

In today's urban wage earning society where women at best earn 68 cents to the male dollar and the only property most couples have is the mortgage on the house, the women and children of Texas are left poorly equipped for economic survival. But a woman who has invested her life in her husband's career gets alimony, right? Not in Texas, it has to be contractual. But a woman is rewarded for services rendered in the course of the marriage, right? Not in Texas. Damages for pain and suffering or loss of consort? Nope. If she put her husband through school she'll get a percentage of future earnings? Not in Texas. If her spouse squandered money she'll be reimbursed? Sorry, a man has a right to squander funds foolishly. But the children will be protected as child support will be indexed to earnings, right? Not in Texas. Not even a tycoon could be forced by the courts to pay more than minimums. College for kids is a given with certain assets, right? Nope. In Texas a child is on his own at 18 even though he's not considered old enough to buy a drink until he's 21.

Why does Texas favor men over women? After all, this was a state where a woman could not own property without the co-signing of a man well into the mid 1960s. The Bubba factor. Who will change the laws, the Texas legislators? Not them big boys. The governor? I'm not holding my breath there. The Texas Bar or Texas Trial Lawyers? No and No. Not until it benefits them financially to do so.

Women in happy marriages are unconcerned; I know, for I was once part of that sorority. Women in unhappy marriages are frightened with good reason. Divorcees are too tired to lead causes. Change will occur, as it usually does, when people get organized and make a noise. There are currently no lobbying groups effecting change. It will probably take the energy and youth of children of divorce who lived through working Mom and Disneyland Dad to make those changes. These kids, probably the daughters, might go to law school and change things.

But if economic parity was truly achieved in divorce, you just might find a few more Texans staying married.

After this article, I was approached by a few civic leaders to lead reforms on divorce laws, to go on a talk show with other doctors' wives, but I was exquisitely attuned to how that would affect my children. I didn't want to become a professional divorcee. I thought I would be able to co-parent and smooth the roiling waters. Didn't happen. Sometimes you can't even lead a horse to water, especially one who is running without a bit.

I was on my knees all the time, going to workshops, retreats, but also ticked off with churches where there were so many ardent churchgoers filled with piety and judgmentalism about broken homes.

Church can be wherever hearts gather *(Hear this Bible Belt)*

Ever hear people in this town talk about going to church or asking you where you attend? It's a loaded question, because there's a church or synagogue on just about every corner and where you go speaks volumes about who you are on a whole lot of levels. Religiosity and self-righteousness have almost nothing to do with the tenets of any of the world's great faiths but have almost everything to do with denominations, factions, and sects. Like rivaling football teams whole congregations are boosters to their beliefs that sanctimoniously set them apart in an especially right relationship with "the Big Guy Upstairs" or at the very least some choose a church so the kids get in the right youth group. Churchaholics abound in this buckle of the Bible belt where attendance is scrupulously noted and dogma is scrutinized for political correctness. It can flat take the spirituality out of faith.

What comprises the best church? I would suggest it is not the cult of personality of this or that rabbi, minister, priest, or pastor. It is not the vestry, elders, brethren or clergy. Neither is it where there is the most emotion, best music or prettiest architecture. Here's church:

A broken woman going through divorce on emotional empty shows up for her son's wrestling match but sits up and off, away from the parents, because she is too stricken to cheer or interact with anyone. She will simply bear witness to her son's effort. A group of fathers supporting the team notices, and without fanfare mounts the bleachers. They sit by her without conversation and simply start loudly cheering on her son. After the match, he looks up seeking out his supporters. He sees. Last year that was church to me.

All those years I had taught Sunday school and Vacation Bible School and been a good girl I now found pastoral care lacking at church. It was not from my clergy I found solace, but from good people, mostly of faith, who just responded. A plane ticket to visit a friend came in the mail. A box of gently used evening dresses for my budding daughter left on my doorstep. A plumber who would not take my money. The traffic court judge in the Bubble, who dismissed my ticket and thanked me for teaching his child in Sunday school. The neighborhood patrolman, who stopped my son speeding with a warning and told him to go home and not worry his mother, who was suffering enough. (It was a small suburb after all.)

Dallas has come a long way in pastoral care, but divorce was off most area churches' radar then. Finally clergy have begun dealing with families as they are instead of how they ought to be, advising people who are in abusive or chaotic relationships to get out. Divorce is not always a tragedy, just a last resort when kids are involved. Maybe some people are terribly mismatched. Or maybe some marriages have a shelf life. I suppose there's that.

1995, *At My House (Just a by-line for my columns, it's just my house now.)*

Well, politics is back in the news with another impending election cycle and so am I. How was your summer and fall? I have tuned out politics after a hiatus only to find out that like a bad soap opera nothing much has changed. The economy and government are still stagnant. Frustration has seeped into our families' daily lives, and threatens our spirits and our communities. The politicians attempt to articulate this frustration with sound bytes, slogans about new beginnings, fairness, and the drumbeat of family values. My kids' constant refrain has been, "Mom get with the 90s" but so far that hasn't been a picnic. This year I'm thinking of sending to everyone I know, especially my Congressmen, the slogan "Get a

Grip."

I do not draw much hope for revitalizing the spirits of Americans from institutions, bureaucracies, or well-funded agencies. We must rediscover our rugged individualism through community bonds, even in zip codes like 90210 or 75205. Look closely at the child who goes through the lunch line looking at the floor, the father who erupts in rage at Little League games, the woman wearing sunglasses in the grocery aisle, the teenager who is always in fights.

As we muddle through mid-life at our house, I am struck how during complicated times there is no quick fix than can get the American family on an even keel. It takes patience, flexibility, communication and an ability to cohere and make concessions. But behind my family's values is always looming the family budget. Certain choices have to be made. You can't live on VISA and debt forever.

Like all families, the American family has got to sit down and look at the family budget. It sets the boundaries for how we can function. Would somebody please tell my crazy Uncle he's a spendaholic and needs help? We need to do a community intervention on him. You may know him. His name is Sam.

The fact is life became a constant scramble to make enough money to keep my kids reasonably parallel to their peers. They definitely did not have a Disneyland Dad. Each held down an after school job. I cast about for how a history major, a former schoolteacher could make money at mid-life. "Sales" was the constant refrain. Stocks, mortgages, or real estate was touted as the most opportune way. What was a right brained verbal romantic going to do in a left brained numbers crunching business world? I could do home repairs, knew the streets of Dallas from carpooling, had moved a bunch, and when a couple of friends approached who were realtors and told me I could do this, I got my license. In fact, I took the exam the day my lawyer called and picked me up spontaneously to prove up the divorce, just as my hot water heater broke and flooded the house that I was putting on the market. The hits just kept on coming.

I begin to recalibrate my life instead of just mourning the old. My widening circle of single ladies gave me a "disengagement" shower complete with lots of bottles of wine, snarky cards, a blow up date, some sexy lingerie for "whenever" and a bag of naughty niceties just in case whenever never came.

Fall 1995, *Dating* (Life just changed cycles)

My daughter and I have both just started car dating. She's 15 and I'm not. My curfew is later than hers but that's not the only problem. I'm not sure which one of us is more uncomfortable with what the other one is doing. It's not that we don't consort with nice people; it's just that she's my only daughter, my baby and as she frequently points out, I'm her single parent mother.

How do you know when you're ready to date? With a teenager it's fairly simple. Bodies bloom, hormones surge, and suddenly there is just no stopping nature. Then there is every parent's struggle to put parameters on courtship. The age-old issues to be grappled with usually involve youth, whiskey, and car keys coupled with burgeoning sexuality. The overriding concern is the safety of the adolescent, so dates are scrutinized not so much for personality as for maturity.

For middle-aged divorced people the lines for dating readiness are more blurred. You're ready for excursions when you can walk into a bookstore without immediately gravitating toward the self-help section, when your life is no longer a Woody Allen movie, when you've moved beyond group therapy, Prozac, and T-shirts with slogans like "I'm low on estrogen and I've got a gun." For some there is the thrill of the chase with Sunday school classes and singles' parties becoming scavenger hunts for mates. At best there are some sorties arranged by friends or which happen serendipitously.

Any way you look at it mid-life dating is freighted with discomfort. All the old familiar teenaged feelings come surging back. Remember clutching popcorn in the movie theatre to avoid the hand holding dilemma? Remember being embarrassed that someone might see you with this person? The awkwardness at the door is compounded when you realize your child may be spying out a window.

With any age there are undercurrents of sexuality. I am conscious of role modeling behavior for my daughter and her older college brothers. I am conscious of how finite my energy level is for a relationship of any kind. I am conscious of the games people play...so perhaps the greatest difference in my daughter's dating and my own is simple awareness.

An old college friend and singer/songwriter from Nashville phoned recently after a hiatus of several years to catch up on this new phase in my life. In her husky Southern voice she sighed, "How ya' doing, hon?" I labored to explain divorce and relationships and this unforeseen turn of events, which defied sound bytes. "I've learned better than to time share a man, and what I want most is for my life not to be so tacky, to feel normal again," I confided.

I've had a lot of advice in the past few years, but hers was the best. "Honey, don't go looking for normal. Normal's just a cycle on a washing machine."

That year I took my teen daughter with friends on a beach trip. They gave me a T-shirt that said, "My Next Husband will be Normal."

SECOND WASH

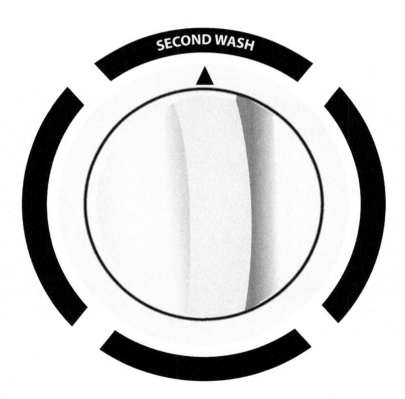

NORMAL'S JUST A CYCLE ON A WASHING MACHINE

Part Four: Second Wash

So begins life anew in a house that has only my name on the mortgage, on my credit cards, and on the signs that hang on my new listings. I had no idea how the business worked. I thought brokers gave agents business, and they gave home tours like docents, and then did some paperwork. People knew I was honest and smart so the business would just pour in, right? It was so much harder than I imagined. Learning new emerging technology, asking people for business, people who were my neighbors and friends, did not come naturally. I was not only horribly self-conscious, but also terrified. My own house was my first listing, and I brought the buyer to our new lake cabin, the one my ex had gotten in the settlement. That was satisfying. I advertised, worked arduous hours, often encountered patronizing behavior by buyers and sellers and still tried to hop around to every kid's event.

With emerging awareness in some ways I became softer, in some ways harder. As some money came in, slowly my photographed smile became less manic; my new world of title people, inspectors, appraisers, lenders, and realtors supplanted my other. My goals were to finish my children's education, minimize their emotional damage, help them fulfill their dreams, hold our remnant together, and be a respected professional until one day I could get back to my passions. The kids shared a beat up old jeep, had their own phone line and, I told them to try to develop whatever relationship they could with their father without my involvement. It's a sad fact that every holiday, every milestone was hard. But humor returns, although never as insouciant. And you don't die from divorce.The opposite of love is not hate, fear, anger...it's indifference.

Later I wondered why I had put myself through all that angst. All those years of feeling a bit guilty for being "just a housewife," but the working world was quickly demystified. Careers are just jobs to feed yourself and family, not your soul. That's your spiritual walk. And it's a solo journey.

May 1994, Press Release: "Associate makes all the right moves. Len Bourland joins real estate firm."

"Len knows more about moving than most. She has lived in a total of three countries, five states, and 17 houses during her life. This is only one of the reasons she will be a success. Her enthusiasm is infectious." My broker to the *Park Cities People*.

Truth is there is nothing funnier or more irreverent than a carload of my realtor friends and broker caravanning around town going through houses. A different kind of carpooling caper from a decade earlier. Restores my sense of humor.

Fall 1996, *Real Estate as Contact Sport: Veterans relate their war stories*

It's a little known fact that the real estate agents are, among other things, family counselors, handymen, housekeepers, and occasionally gymnasts. It is a rare agent who has not picked up dog poop on the carpet, made up a bed or thrown dishes in the dishwasher, held a cranky baby so mommy could run upstairs and peek back at a master bath, or helped defuse a squabble developing with a client couple over money. Talk to veteran agents and it's usually a walk on the *Far Side* with encounters into every conceivable situation.

One of my fellow agents remembers the time she went to preview a vacant new build when, upon entering with her keypad, she heard frantic pounding. Another agent had gone through the house hours earlier, decided to "powder her nose" but once inside the new bath found the interior door handle had not been installed. This was

121

before portable phones, and she was locked in. Others have walked in on couples between the sheets while showing a house, while many a realtor has had to shadow those people who wander through open houses with "sticky" fingers.

The nadir of my own experience may have been the couple being transferred who showed up to house hunt with their four children…who had chickenpox. Or it may have been the empty nesters who insisted I blast the television while playing the piano downstairs as they went to the upstairs master to check the noise level and soundproofing. As I glumly plunked out "Chopsticks," the homeowner's parrot came to life squawking obscenities, loudly in my face.

Stories of being locked in or out of houses abound, but a fellow agent may top the list. This lady was attired in her suit and heels to show important clients a large stately home. Her key wouldn't work the deadbolt in front so she dashed around to the back door to let her people in the gracious front entry. She encountered a locked back gate. Gamely this agent threw her shoes over the fence and attempted to climb over. At the moment she landed she knew she had broken or sprained her ankle. Then the sprinkler system turned on. She ended up having to crawl soaking wet back to her horrified clients to have them take her to the emergency room. The agent shall remain nameless, as she has already suffered enough.

In my case of the inevitable lockout, some clients wandered upstairs as I went outside to turn on a fountain in an enclosed courtyard when I heard the sickening click of an automatic lock. I spied a ladder left by yardmen, scurried up the ten-foot wall, leapt onto the hood of a parked SUV on the other side; then shoes in hand, I returned through the front door, my clients none the wiser.

My cheerleading gymnast days stood me well. Real estate. It's also a contact sport.

Yet as a single working mother what ensues are a lot of columns about money, consumerism, taxes, as this preoccupies me on a daily basis, interspersed with musings on the kids, culture and an occasional romance.

Fall 1996, *Picture This (Excesses of high school party weekends)*

I've just returned from picking up the photos of the homecoming dance, spending just under twenty bucks. This memorabilia was the cherry on the sundae for a North Dallas high school party weekend, which my friends in other cities tell me is quite the norm. We spent weeks searching for the holy grail of the dress, one nobody else would have. The price tag was the same as my wedding dress. It sits in a puddle on the floor, probably never to be worn again. Then came the shoes, boutonniere for her date, and the cost of body maintenance. She had a mani/pedi, her hair styled, but I drew the line at the tanning salon. Cash outlay: a lot. Her date took her to the nicest restaurant in the city, sent her roses, bought the tickets, but I nixed a limo. I did not allow the ubiquitous hotel after-party or the newest craze, co-ed spend the night parties arranged by parents at somebody's lake house or ranch in an attempt to circumvent the local post-party drinkathons. This hoopla was not for a bride or debutante or senior prom queen but for a garden variety homecoming dance in this her second year of high school; and there will be many other such weekends.

I am happy for my daughter, like her brothers before her, to dress up, to receive "star" treatment, to court, to experience the best life has to offer, to fit in with her peers, to have happy memories; and I remember well what teenagers do.

I have terrific kids. I also have consumer junkies. They are addicted to a lifestyle of conspicuous consumption along with their peer group, feel deserving of it, and have been enabled to do so by parents. The rest of the parents in this community are my fellow pushers. I fear for what it will take for these kids to be happy in their 30s, 40s, 50s. You know you're getting old when you start sentences with "When I was a kid..." but when I was a kid, mothers, none of whom worked, were ever involved in the dances. Older students threw out some crepe paper in the gym, we put on our prom clothes, danced to a band, and as I recall, we had a good time. This was at an elite Atlanta private school. Fathers didn't finance extravaganzas.

What if next year for homecoming we had a street dance, (cost the band), a giant co-ed slumber party in the football stadium, charged $100 (savings huge), took the money and the next day built a house for Habitat and called it Coming Home?...The parents could even get involved.

December 1996, *Ask the Kids (What they really want isn't pricey)*

As soon as the turkey's picked off the bird, the Cowboys have played, and the names have been put in the pot to fish out for Christmas gifts, the great bustle begins: Christmas shopping. Every year I promise myself to cut back, and every year I end up buying and wrapping. Remembrances are great, the merchants need our business, and presents are fun.

And yet, I was amused on more than one level when the husband of one friend got a hearty chuckle at a holiday party recently, when he announced that all that his wife wanted for Christmas was the gift that couldn't be exchanged, "Grow up before the kids do."

The proverbial mid-life crisis stories then ensued.

It is true that there are periods in life when it seems that we attend a lot of funerals, worry enormously about our taxes and pension plans, and expend all our energy just meeting the demands of everyday life. Christmas shopping becomes just another problem to be solved. It seems women scurry off to plastic surgeons, and men rush off to buy sports cars and people jog and jog and jog. I think the underlying premise is that somehow youth or feeling young is the antidote to the enormous responsibilities and mountain of stuff that seems to weigh us down.

Yet what the young embrace is not the lifestyle or the freedom from responsibility, it is an attitude about life that we allow to slip away and is relatively inexpensive. It is the wonder, the awe, and delight in the journey of life as a magical mystery tour that the young and the young at heart share. Consider the responses from college kids on the Internet in what is a natural high:

"Clean sheets. Tailgating on a warm Saturday. Laughing 'til your face hurts. Falling asleep in the sun on a cool day. Daydreaming. Going dancing. Giggling. When a dog jumps in your face because it's happy to see you. Watching a candle burn. Walking barefoot in the sand. Blowing bubbles. Screaming at the top of your lungs. Sleeping under heavy covers on a cold rainy day. Fresh flowers. Seeing your family after so long. Kissing in the rain. Rollercoasters. Drinking a cold beer with Mexican food. Walking out of your last final. Oreo ice cream. Skinny-dipping. Hot chocolate. Pillows. Hearing someone say, "I miss you" and know they mean it. Singing in the shower. Realizing this is who ya' are, where ya' wanna be, and who ya' wanna spend it with."

Could we just wrap that up and put it under the tree?

Or cash. My kids always wanted that. I was long past making them write thank you notes for warm ups in the wrong sizes without tags for returning in unmarked boxes from relatives who had gone to a local discount

127

mall. I appealed for books if not gift certificates. We gave each other lottery tickets. They had girlfriends or a boyfriend by now. So much for traditions. Some years we went to Christmas Eve service, some years we had a morning brunch and played monopoly. Life in flux was our only constant.

January 1997, *How to Survive the College Daze*

There is no such thing as college kids slipping silently back home. They travel in thundering herds. Their evenings begin just about the time their parents are going to bed. Phones ring all night long as one heard attempts to round up a maverick and thinks nothing of trying the (sleeping) parent's line if the student line doesn't answer. There is nothing parents love more than having their college kids come home from school except possibly having them go back. I've had nights when one slammed in about 4 a.m. in a tux while another left soon after to go hunting. I quit setting the alarm system, as they would just crawl on the roof and go through windows.

With two college sons, I have come home from the office only to find dead ducks in the sink from the bird hunters still sprawled in camo gear, snoring on sofas with empties on the coffee table alongside cups of tobacco juice. Pieces from tuxedos from the other son's gang are still strewn about as well. The air-conditioning is set on an energy efficient 50 degrees. Mothers of college girls tell me it is no different, just different stuff. The kitchen is a war zone. Planning is impossible. I have also returned home to find an army sipping my best chardonnay, devouring yesterday's leftovers, along with tonight's spaghetti and tomorrow's tamales with a couple of boxes of cereal.

The other day at exercise I spied a friend frantically running on the treadmill. It seems her college kid was a straggler. I suggested blasting religious music, disconnecting the cable, and running the weedeater under his bedroom window early in the mornings to get him motivated to get back to school. She looked dubious until I reminded her there were less than 100 days to spring break.

February 1997, *Takers (Was I ever just a naïve housewife?)*

Someone at the dinner party threw out yet another alarming statistic from a recent poll that showed our continuing moral decline: only 32% of school age children knew the Golden Rule. That's not "He who has the Gold rules" but "Do unto others as you would have them do unto you." The table of baby boomers erupted in corroborating evidence.

A doctor, who had done *pro bono* work for a patient and saved his life, was then sued by the man's family for some perceived lack of care.

As a realtor who works on straight commission to support myself, I trumped this. I had been showing houses for months to a young couple, spending hours of my time even though they were not buying much. I ran market analyses, educated them about market trends, took their calls at all hours and showed them many, many homes. One weekend they went out and bought direct from a For Sale By Owner using my information and sample forms. The irony is the seller would have paid a commission anyway. After going behind me, they telephoned. They wanted to know if they'd gotten a good deal!

An interior designer had a similar story involving fabric swatches and room designs, when the young people just took her ideas and went out and copied them, doing it themselves. They ordered furniture from her, and then decided they didn't want it after all and refused to pay. She ended up in small claims court.

In each case professionals had not only their

skills but also time stolen. Maybe this isn't a sign of moral decline, and it has been this way from *Genesis* to *Canterbury Tales*. Perhaps we boomers, the generation who produced the narcissistic flower children and hippies who occupied buildings and destroyed professors' research have just become aware of how the world works for some of the young, with our accumulated life experiences. Still, oh for that Golden Rule.

When this piece was published the Dow had just broken through to a new record high.... 7000. And I was (ugh) trying to figure out how to manage my money. That's a never-ending saga.

February 1997, *Yow the Dow (Financial planning, gambling right?)*

Long ago in a galaxy far, far away I was a college student majoring in history with minors in French and art. Although it was a liberal arts university, my father fretted I was not majoring in something useful. There were no courses offered in interior design, or journalism; that was what you did at state schools; he meant like economics. That had no thrall for me with things like mathematical models, probability and statistics, all things that made my eyes glaze over. Stuff guys liked. I mentioned law school later but that was not in my parents' economics for me.

A quarter of a century later, I realize that I still have my critical thinking skills from history, *n'est ce pas*, and all those econ majors were learning about was how to gamble. Look at the Dow. It seems that the little graph in the business section of the paper is studied like tea leaves and entrails of yore by none other than, economists. And what they're divining is making people nervous. The Dow's too high. The economy is overheated. The market needs a correction. Too much money is pouring in. It's like 1929 before the Crash.

Nope. With someone who has a couple of degrees in American history, let me tell you what the market is like: the ponies. The mutual fund analysts' and economists' forecasts have all the scientific weight of an exacta or trifecta pick. That's why all those boys in college went into economics. They were just trying to glean tips for the football pools and greensheets. Economists and players in the stock market are betting men.

The most powerful man in the world last week was sexless, frumpy, owlish Alan Greenspan. When the Chairman of the Fed hiccups, the world's economic markets rattle. But I'm feeling confident. Why?

Because Alan said so. You betcha.

I'd just gotten an award for a column I wrote chastising Hillary for tolerating Bill after Monica. I wanted her to toss the man, his sax, the infamous necktie into a garbage bag in the Rose Garden and send him packing to Camp David. How I still get ticked at those cheating hearts!

May 1997, *The Donald, Miss Universe and the Clintons*

It's that time of year for endings and beginnings, weddings, graduations, and new careers. So it's a fitting time for what we all knew would happen is happening. The Donald and Marla are splitting, and as usual, the timing is magnificent. Big Donald is dumping Marla just before his net worth may double or triple again...something about his casinos. It will be friendly, however, because both got what they wanted. He got a trophy wife, and she got fame and money.

Marla supposedly will only get about three million, about one for each year of the marriage, but there will be lots of child support for their appropriately named daughter, Tiffany. Plus Marla can trade on her Barbie doll looks as long as she stays in shape, and she's probably not going back to Albany, Georgia to open a fitness center.

Of course the Trumps want the press to ignore the story and give them privacy. (Yeah, right. This from a guy who once had girlfriend, Marla hovering about Aspen with wife Ivana schussing down the slopes with the paparazzi right behind.) The Donald released this story now so the press could cover more important news, like the upcoming Miss Universe Pageant. That's the televised beauty contest the Donald bought and is rumored to be having Marla emcee with her considerable talent.

Will Ivana and Marla start doing lunch to speculate on who the third Mrs. Donald will be? Will Marla reveal during commercial pageant breaks what career she will pursue? It is rumored Donald is dieting and losing weight. Will the pageant contestants be hoping to be crowned the next Mrs. Trump as he surveys the talent? Given his penchant for blondes will the Scandanavian gals have better odds?

I predict The Donald will soon be squiring around a beauty queen under the age of 25 and maybe honeymooning in the Lincoln bedroom since the Clintons offer it to big donors. One day they may even get married. Stay tuned for the next installment on that continuing

American soap, "Trump."

By now my boys are well ensconced in college, my daughter is doing her level best to spend all her time out of the house, and I need a break. But I realize that I am, if not serene, actually happy and regaining confidence.

May 1997, *Proud Tina Keeps on Burning* (*A gal's gotta rock some*)

The kid sacking groceries shook his head in amazement and turned to a buddy, "How could that lady buy a birthday cake and just walk out and leave it" he snickered.

"It's easy," I blurted out as I wheeled around and looked him levelly in the eye. "She's got a lot going on. She'll be back in an hour and retrieve it."

Ah, youth. In the last week I've lost my car keys, ditto sunglasses. When I retrace my steps to stores inevitably they pull out a drawers with dozens of keys and sunglasses. Small consolation. Maybe it's mid-life crisis, or hormones, or divorce or whatever.

So last week I joined some of my fellow sisters and went to hear that dynamo of rock and soul that can flat recharge a gal's batteries. I've been a Tina Turner fan since the dark ages, before I could really understand her lyrics but just liked the beat and singing along. Recently when I was singing along with an oldie but goody my college son had shushed me. I protested this was my music and I knew it the way he did his heavy metal. He protested that I may have lived in the 60s but he knew the 60s music, because he had taken a rock music course at Texas and was "into" it. No way. I went to this concert to sing.

Got a crappy job? Kids messed up? Heartaches and dead ends? Mean mama? Well, take a load off because Tina's been there, and you can feel it the minute she strides out and wails, "What's love got to do with it?"

Oprah, the talk show queen and richest woman in showbiz has been touring with Tina, making not so famous Tina's queen for a day with giveaways: cars, trips, college educations for women striving to rebound from abusive relationships. Her generosity is impressive. Yet when Tina is onstage she becomes the Queen of our Hearts. "Proud Mary Keep on Burning" could be renamed "Proud Tina, Ike You're History."

Tina lives it. If she hadn't existed we would have had to invent her.

August 1997, *Patch, Patch, Patch* *(It all falls apart)*

This is a short quiz so just go with your gut here. Which is more annoying: a) car maintenance b) home maintenance c) body maintenance d) technical maintenance.

For some that might be a matter of cost, for others, age, for yet others, timing. Few teenagers worry about a sore shoulder or stomachache but it might cause an elderly person night terrors. A fender bender might instill terror into a young person who depends on the car for a new job or a teen borrowing the family car while it's just a nuisance to a harassed housewife on her to do list. College kids aren't loosing sleep over the washing machine breaking down but to a young mommy with toddlers in cold weather it's a nightmare. No air conditioning is dreaded in the heat of Texas but it's devastating for a wedding planner. And nobody likes his TV, phone or computer to seize up.

So last week, when my moaning college kid who was recovering from knee surgery felt a drip from the cow's udder in the den ceiling over the bathroom, I knew I needed the plumber. My other collegiate announced he needed a brake job before he returned to Austin the next day and couldn't get in for service, so he might need to swap cars and come back in a week if I would get his fixed in the interim. My daughter then breezed in with a laundry list of all the items she needed to start high school the next day, everything from a trig calculator to a crucial haircut appointment and asked if she could borrow my phone. That's the phone I had not had time to get to the AT&T store to figure out how to unlock it and how that had even happened. Meanwhile my pager was going off. Just then we all heard a boom. There was construction in the neighborhood and a transformer had just blown. The lights dimmed.

So the answer to the quiz of which repairs are the biggest nuisance or the most essential? Sometimes it's the time honored answer e) all of the above.

Keep selling those houses and don't ever fantasize about fabulous bathrooms. I get so heartily weary, rhapsodizing over marble, granite, and designer stoves. It just made me dig in the dirt and plant flowers in my yard. My kids keep me both crazy and sane.

October 1997, *Batten down the hatches, it's Texas-OU weekend*

The lines at Sam's have been long, with folks stocking up on the supplies, cups, plates, drinks, and lots of party food. Mothers of college age men and women are reminded of when their kids were toddlers as they are having to put up valuables or anything breakable of value. They're also trying to get as much sleep as possible just like during those nap times of yesteryear. That's because this Saturday is rivaled only by the mall madness the day after Thanksgiving and Christmas Eve at DFW airport.

To all who have migrated to Big D from Seattle or Boston or a foreign country these next few days are a tribal rite, Texas-OU weekend, or to a minority OU-Texas weekend. Throw in the State Fair and high school Friday night lights and the only thing to do is buckle up for the carnival. Everybody who is not a stranger in town (if they could possibly find a hotel room) knows to pick up dry-cleaning, make grocery runs, and stay off the streets. Traffic is in gridlock and all those orange cones and barricades in our never ending road construction will not mean detour to orange hungry Longhorn fans, any more than red lights mean stop to the Sooners.

Last year was the year of the Winnebago when my senior Longhorn showed up in front of my house in an RV the entire length of my front footage with several of his fellow frat brothers and their dates. Nobody (including me) would allow them to park in my driveway or any parking lot. Nor would I let them use the bathrooms since the previous year a gang of boys' dates used all my towels, flooded the upstairs bathroom which required a plumber, and stole my hairdryer while most of my makeup disappeared. Instead I gave them supplies and herded them on. So for 48 hours the Moveable Feast crawled the streets of Dallas with a rotating shift of drivers. The husbands of friends went inside to take a peek and came away not a little impressed and jealous. We've gone from the Fort in our garage to the four wheeled Fort in only a little over a decade.

Then interspersed with kids and work were the sporadic dates. Sometimes the dates were so bad I would set my pager off, back when realtors, doctors, and workmen wore them in the Jurassic Era of technology. There was the guy whose name was Leon and started off with, "Know what the difference between me and you is?" He made the universal sign for ok. "Get it? The letter O and also zero. Leon, Len. We're perfect." I mumbled it was a nickname from Ellen while I set my beeper off.

Or the guy at the bar who kept saying, "Barkeep, Yo Cap'n, another round here, hit me pal." Nonstop this as he got sloshed and slammed his ex wife whom I knew.

Lucky gal to escape him. Beep beep. Off went my beeper. Or the Romeo, who, when I asked him what he liked to do crowed, "You mean after making love on every beach in the world with a beautiful woman like you!" What movie had he gotten that line from? Beep, beep. Oops Gotta go. A contract just came in. Or the divorced pastor turned stockbroker who took me to Souper Salad for lunch, grabbed my hand and prayed endlessly as a smirking hardhat outside the window fired up his jackhammer. Beep beep. Gotta make this quick.

There was the lothario who reached across the console of his Jag, squeezed my inner thigh and winked, "We're going to have a good time!" while I removed his paw, put it on the steering wheel and flatly told him he would need both hands for driving. Then I reached in my purse and set off my beeper. Umm, must be a client calling. Or Mr. Jack the elderly guy whose family had taken away his car keys but got out in his yard across the street and did jumping jacks shirtless whenever I went to my car. My daughter laughed hysterically when she found a typed letter on onionskin paper asking me to meet him at a restaurant (that had piano music). He would send a cab for me.

By now if my life were a Hollywood film, I would

have been realtor of the year, started my own agency, been on Oprah and had Robert Redford on my doorstep. My daughter asked why my dates were so unattractive. I reminded her they looked just like her friends' dads, who did not look like Robert Redford either. Nor was I everyman's dream. This short, Type A gal would never be languid, mysterious, serene...or buxom.

Spring 1998, *The Oenophile (What to order on a date)*

One of the worst parts of dating at mid-life is having a waiter in a restaurant come over and ask to take your wine order. Depending on the date, the caliber of the restaurant, and the menu, this is a moment of truth or consequences.

There are the befuddled gents who ask, "What would you like?" Pressure. I take the coward's way out and order the house this or that. There was a Supreme Court Justice who once said he couldn't define pornography, but he knew it when he saw it. I feel that way about wine. At the grocery that's about a 12 to 15 dollar bottle of wine which doesn't coat my mouth after the meal. I've come a long way from when I was a bride who liked my grape based on the shape of the bottle: Mateus or Chianti in the cute straw orbs. But I am nowhere near, nor do I ever hope to be, like the oenophiles who pour over the wine list like Holy Scripture. Few of my dates (*Bachelor Bob, Dennis the Date, Stan the Man, everybody got a nickname*) cared about wine except for the price tag. Nobody lasted more than a couple of dates, especially since my embarrassed high school daughter usually refused to answer the door if I was upstairs drying my hair...while sipping some fortifying refrigerator house wine.

She graduates from high school with top grades, a homecoming princess, and I am so grateful to her college brothers, the ones who teased her mercilessly as a little girl, but now come home to glare at her boyfriends and crunch their hands at the door. My dream is to get her to Paris somehow, someway. She has turned down my alma mater to go to The University, and I want her to know it's a big planet out there.

June 1998, *Paris in the Summer...When it Sizzles* (*Le bon voyage*)

Back before the Age of Passports, circa pre-World War I, Americans who could went abroad to round out their education. Everyone more or less gets the picture thanks to the movie, Titanic. On a much lesser scale, which included AAdvantage miles and a friend's cheap apartment, I just took my recent high school grad to the grandest city in the world in an effort to ensure that she does not believe that the world begins in Highland Park and ends in Austin at The University. I could not wait to show her Paris...France that is. I wanted to see the Champs Elysee mirrored in her eyes, the grandiose Louvre flood her emotions, the sensual fragrances and culinary experiences permeate her being. I thought she might even appreciate her mother's ability to navigate her through uncharted waters thanks to my college French and my own semester abroad in that charming country. A mother/daughter bonding trip, *n'est ce pas?*

Reality. She's grown up in North Dallas. She kept looking for Paris chic on the streets, and on the whole, she thought the people ill-clad with bad skin and bad teeth. She quickly noticed there were no nail boutiques on every street corner making her wonder aloud who came up with the term "French manicure." The realization that deodorant is not as highly valued along with the lack of air-conditioning made her underwhelmed by the perfumes as a whole. She understood why people were strong of body odor after riding the on subway system, which she admired for economy and efficiency but found rather rank.

Nevertheless, she became fluent in reading the Metro map and making changes as I pondered interchanges endlessly in my estrogen-deprived moments.

"It's why you're no good on the Internet, Mom."

While I waxed on and on about the quality of French garments, food, and art she noticed that most people in the Metro wore Nikes or clearly envied hers, listened to Rap or Hip Hop and went to dubbed American movies. She found French plumbing barbaric and thought the little telephone handle type shower the principal flaw in Parisian hygiene.

I quickly realized that the days I had mapped out for us were impossible. Despite Stairmaster and Nautilus, my muscles and joints screamed at the constant walking. Moreover, I had not figured on the World Cup Soccer tournament. Paris was like a combination of the Superbowl and Mardi Gras. I fought crowds to see "my Paris."

When my daughter ran into high school friends she proceeded to boogie on without me with her *tres cheres amies*, while I escaped the mob by discovering the flea market of Clignancourt, the food market on the Rue Mouffetard, the new Picasso Museum in the Marais, the romantic Montmartre Cemetery, all away from the hub

145

along the banks of the Seine. My daughter also adores Paris. It's a town that knows how to throw one hell of a street party and serves up great wine, no ID required. So we've bonded on being Francophiles.

C'est la vie.

Now that the kids were gone for the summer and I was coming up on 50, I had my first serious romance. Finally! When Joe takes me on a trip to the Carolinas the infatuation bleeds through. Read between the lines.

July 1998, *Passion*

Passion. Sometimes it's fiery and hot and explosive, but it can be as light and cool and refreshing as a Carolina mountain breeze. That's how it was last week in a packed college auditorium at the summer arts festival in the Appalachian hills of Boone, North Carolina in the form of aging folk singer, John McCutcheon. This gentle soul soon had us in rounds rubbing, tapping, and clapping our hands. We laughed and sang not to make him feel good, but because it made us feel good. And as we responded we learned wise lessons.

With moistened eyes, and lumpy throats we erupted into wild applause and clamored for an encore, before reverting back into heat-crazed, fractious travelers. We were not merely entertained that summer afternoon, we were welded together by a man who makes his passion the gentle art of song.

This long distance romance didn't last but a year but was nice to feel coupled, if only for awhile. He was a creative guy who had written and produced some movies; it was a pleasant interlude.

August 1998, *Boys fly away, Girls soar gently (Empty nest)*

When my son went to college several years ago, he pointed his pickup truck toward Austin, tossed in about ten garbage bags filled with clothes, some frayed towels, a couple of sets of sheets (which it turned out was one too many), all his shoes and said, "See ya'." That's it. No maudlin hugs, no tears, no big speech. Once there he didn't make his grades first semester, did a stint at the local community college, grew up by fits and starts and ultimately graduated and moved on. I never moved him into dorm rooms or apartments, or made beds ("Mom, don't bother"). I think he vacuumed his sheets (and I am not making this up) every now and then, tossed them out at semester and put on the other set. His dorm room was laden with clothes in piles. "Don't touch anything, Mom!" It seemed he had a system: one pile for clean, one dirty and one in between. After obtaining his sheepskin, he passed on the ceremony, got a job and became a successful "bidness" man.

Today with a lump in my throat and aching muscles I have returned from that same university having deposited my Highland Park Princess and baby. The difference was at least from Mars to Venus. She won't be going to community college; she's an organized student who had files and lists just to orchestrate her transition to college living. She co-ordinated the Ralph Lauren bedding ensemble with her roommates, which involved many phone calls and white sales. She packed her clothes in plastic containers marked seasonally and by style (party, class, sports etc).

What went to college kept proliferating like kudzu. During the summer my living room was the depository for her stuff: shoe racks, shelving units, personal computer, lockbox, bath, laundry and personal essentials, monogrammed towels, closet organizer, study lamps...you get the picture. There no room for evening dresses or evening wear; they would be shipped or delivered by people doing the Dallas/Austin axis. We packed a Suburban to the gills, and we are people on a tight budget. My child was far from elaborate when we arrived. After all, we had not hired a decorator or had furniture made for her room.

When I went to what is considered a prestigious college, Vanderbilt, I brought an electric typewriter; my roomie brought a clock radio and a hi-fi. We went to K-Mart and bought color coordinated nylon orange and gold bedspreads and study pillows to match our drab brownish dorm curtains. We put a year's worth of clothes into small closets and one dresser. During the summer, all our goods except for clothes were stored in metal garbage cans with padlocks in the school basement, as we all lived too far away for weekend jaunts home.

When I got to Austin, I joined the cadre of parents who worked. We elevated beds so storage units could be stowed. We hung shelves and rearranged furniture. We made trips to the hardware store in triple digit heat, made drug store runs and sent out for fast food. The girls milled around while we were hanging clothes. After all rush started the next day. While we toiled away for the young lasses we were diapering in 1980 during Jimmy Carter's Iranian hostage crisis, we did so gratefully and with moistened eyes.

Because our daughters, unlike our sons, let us.

I am the lady sobbing all the way back from Austin, when a concerned truck driver honked me over to to inquire if I was ok. Well mostly. I actually returned home to a son who appeared and wanted help writing a resume. There's always the next thing.

October 1998, *(The Beginning of)* **Cellular Prison**

Seems quaint now but cell phones as necessities began that year.

My cell phone died about three weeks ago and it's like losing dentures and glasses to be without. I use one daily in my business so I'm having a hard time functioning.

"We don't stock that battery any more. The product's just too old."

In other words cellular phones are designed to become functionally obsolescent so that you'll have to buy the newer (more expensive) improved technology after two years. Forget the Presidential scandal. The entire stock market is actually being fueled by the cell phone. All those hi-tech stocks, which drive the mutual funds, depend on these gizmos. Once everyone has gone from digital to analog, we'll have another dip until another, even smaller, even glitzier phone comes out. And have it we must. Because cell phones are cool. My daughter came home from college and immediately demanded a cell phone for her purse.

"How do you expect me to be safe on the highway or going to the library at night!" she challenged.

It seems that cell phones are the latest accessory for a well-dressed co-ed. This was confirmed when a dozen of her friends trooped through my front door with the apparatus attached to ears, noisily telling someone they were now at my house. I have to say it felt fairly prestigious. People are now busy chatting it up in grocery store aisles, football stadiums, on escalators in the mall, as well as in the car.

A caveat about rate plans and that's the use of the word "free" as in free minutes. Under any rate plan with any telecommunications carrier there is absolutely nothing that is "free."

Within months my entire family is living on our cell phones. And soon the rest of the world as well.

December 1999, *Vegas (Merry Christmas kids)*

Having just returned from my first (and probably last) trip to Las Vegas, I can attest to the fact that Elvis is alive and well there. Actually he's all over that town. I took my kids there this year because I refuse to be holiday compliant. I did not get asthma buying a tree, lose my love for mankind in Christmas traffic, have the anxiety of getting the house decorated, or get the flu from trying to overdo to make everyone happy by doing the divorcees' holiday two step. Instead of any guilt trip, I just handed my young adult kids envelopes with the only gift they truly love, cash, and headed for the place that sucks it right out. It seemed only fitting that we went to the city that has embodied what the twentieth century has been about: consumerism. Vegas is about money, risk, odds, technology, and entertainment. In other words it's like the stock market.

My gift to my hard working 20 something kids was some serious playtime. My gift to myself was to do something different and watch them play. I had never wanted to go to Sin City but thought it might be a memorable Christmas. It was. Plus we were back just in time to get to Christmas Eve Church for the spiritual dimension for rounding out the holidays. My resolution for this Y2K is to try to keep life balanced. For behind all the bright lights of the Vegas strip are some really beautiful mountains and sunsets.

My oldest son is going off on his own as a graduate who is now in the working world. Yet I struggle to find ways to keep a semblance of family for my daughter who is still in college and has just broken up with her boyfriend. Plus I miss seeing my children play. I always loved that. When the world hasn't crashed with the overhyped Y2K and my wounded heart has healed, I gambled on Vegas for fun.

Soon after, one of my sons has broken up with a relationship. We're all single now and back out there.

March 2000, *Dating* (Again sigh)

My three kids and I share one thing in common besides the same last name. We all date. I don't think any of us likes is all that much. Dating is one of those things you slog through until you finally find someone whose company you really enjoy. At best it's sort of amusing and breaks the monotony of being with the same gender all the time; at worst it's absolutely painful. The only reason to rotate evenings out is to meet someone whose chemistry is such that you'd like to get to know that person and be in a relationship. Actually that relationship part may be a girl thing. As my daughter and I have concluded, guys want action. They want someone they can do stuff with. Girls want to share. Guys hate that phrase, "We need to talk…"

As a fellow I once dated announced, "If you want somebody to 'share' with, get a girlfriend."

Hmmm. Dating can be so awkward for some, that it may explain why Rick Rockwell and Darva Conger decided to fast forward past it and go right to the altar on the new reality TV show "Who Wants to Marry a Millionaire?"

Dating is expensive. Just ask any guy. Despite gender parity, it's still the guy who does most of the asking and paying. So a male has to really, really be attracted to a member of the opposite sex to start that chase. According to all these surveys, guys usually figure out if they like a girl in about 15 minutes. For girls it takes a whole hour as she is busy "relating" for an additional 45 minutes just to make sure that the attraction isn't merely physical.

There's the "how much does he make?" issue, the cynics would sneer. So when the Fox television producers came up with the crazy notion of having a guy who could not only afford to date, but also hook up with (i.e. marry) a woman in sort of a beauty contest in only one game show, it probably made perfect sense to the guy. He got to pick out a chick from a lineup of gals who were not only willing to don wedding gowns, but bathing suits just like in the Miss America competition. Naturally. the wedding would take place in Las Vegas…every bimbo's idea of heaven. Naturally, the guy picked a bleached blonde. Of course, this wasn't about sex and money for the contestants Rick and Darva. This was about television and fame. Or the real currency of today: celebrity-hood.

Twenty million Americans tuned in to watch Rick Rockwell select his dream date/fiancée, Barbie doll from the line-up last week. Only three million tuned in to watch the Presidential candidates debate. While I missed the show, I couldn't help but learn all about it, as it seemed to be all that was on the news last week. If there was a war or a breaking story it just didn't make the magazines or TV. It was all about That Show and the failed honeymoon where Darva wouldn't sleep with Rick when she immediately realized she'd made "a mistake." That $35,000 engagement ring couldn't take the sting out of the fact that Rick had a past, and not all that much money either. Darva earnestly told Diane Sawyer about how she was a "victim."

Last week one couple without so much as a thin

veneer of caring for each other went after sex and money. It turned out neither got either, although they may have gotten something more: notoriety. In the meantime, the American public got treated to what my kids and I have all experienced…a disastrous blind date.

Mostly though life wasn't about dates. It was about friends, kids, writing, work, trips, the news, exercise, books, volunteer work, spiritual retreats. That was all about love too though, right?

May 2000, *Ahh Love (Mom, how do you know?)*

There is something unnerving about getting an invitation to your college son's childhood, best friend's wedding. This thick vellum envelope was from a child whom I was carpooling to soccer games and ballroom dancing not very long ago; and like my own late bloomer, he was disinterested in girls and was still going trick or treating on Halloween as late as the seventh grade. Could this little towhead, Jack, who had moved to Houston several years ago, the year after he almost burned down my garage smoking his first cigarette, really be tying the knot? What is the world coming to when children are getting married? The world is going round, of course, as it always has. Ah, Love.

"Mom, do you think it will last? I mean he doesn't even have a job or anything, and I know I'm not ready to get married." (Phew.)

Certainly age is not the criterion for an enduring relationship, I assured my man-child. I myself marched down the aisle as a bridesmaid seven times before I graduated from college and six of those unions still endure past the quarter century mark. Nor would I begin to speculate on compatibility as opposites can work as well as compliments or supplements it seems. But chiefly it is the worry in my son's voice that I detect which affects me. Both of my soldiering age boys have struggled with feelings over serious romantic interests, and this question is not trivial. For a family which has survived a divorce there are no homilies or cute family bromides to impart to the next generation like, "Oh honey, you'll know just like your Daddy and I did when...etc."

Fear of failure, fear of pain is a constant undertow in the first waves of new love and affection, clouding all that confused happiness. Like picking daisies out of mud puddles, I want to share what is best about marriage and partnership without sentimentalizing romance or cautioning too much about the pitfalls of life.

My son wants to know how to make love last, not how to make a legal partnership endure; for it is more than mere longevity about his friend's nuptials which is implicit in his question to me. My first instinct is to proffer the advice of wise counsel. Respect and common courtesy, old-fashioned manners are basic to love. The very best behavior exhibited by someone will be during courtship, and if it's not there then, it will not be manufactured later. Predicated on respect is the ability to listen to a mate with intensity, without attempting to turn the conversation back to yourself. This is closely followed by acting on what is heard, exhibiting care and thoughtfulness. Finally, a person who loves is not ambivalent about his or her feelings, but is committed to the other person to the exclusion of all others. This is not at all the same thing as passion, falling in love, attraction, or just plain fun companionship, which are all precursors to this deeper more mature love. And because attraction is so powerful, in order to know if it is capable of sustaining a life partner, there is the difficult but necessary dimension of time, which is so at odds with the urgency of passion and romance. Then these behaviors need to be marinated and confirmed by family, friends and the community as a whole.

But as I survey this young man commencing his third decade of life, I realize I do not wish to preach; rather my wish for him is simple awareness. I know better than to hope for a life without travails for my children; yet it is my earnest desire that each meets the challenges along the way fortified in a loving and intimate partnership.

So instead, I smiled and replied, "I don't have a crystal ball. Will the marriage last? It might. If they both work at it. Do you want to give his old tennis racket back as a wedding present?"

Life has a certain wistfulness. My daughter takes my advice to go abroad as I did, my oldest son is working, my younger son is happy and doing incredibly well in college. So I close on a real estate deal and treat myself to a trip.

October 2000, *Go to Tuscany to Escape Bush/Gore*

After an all too brief ten days of traveling to Italy to visit my college daughter who is studying abroad, I came away with that wonderful benefit: perspective. Driving through Tuscany is breathing in silvery olive groves, spicy cypress trees, sun drenched vineyards, soaking in the tawny ochers, soft umbers, mellow salmons of *residenzas* and *palazzos* and buildings surrounding sun charming *palazzos*. Traveling to Italy is always my idea of a fabulous getaway. But going on break two weeks before a Presidential election is definitely the time to leave the country. No debates, no talk shows, no spinning, no yard signs, no headlines, and a respite from this election's new low, the barrage of nasty e-mails circulated by zealous partisans of both persuasions.

Perhaps the greatest benefit of travel is not only the inevitable adventures, charting new territory, discovering a wonderful bottle of local wine in Montalcino or a little known Piero Della Francesco fresco in Cortona; or misadventures, how to pump diesel gas into an Italian stick shift car at an out of the way pump, how to navigate the maze of outlet shopping in Montevarchi, or how to work the lights in some *pensiones*, but also acquired life wisdom. It's realizing that there is a ton of people on the planet and a lot of them were in Italian museums and churches during the papal Year of the Jubilee. Nobody, not one person, was discussing the Bush/Gore election. Not one tourist standing in line. No taxi driver asked about it. Not one Italian newspaper had anything about in the headlines. Given the fever pitch of this race it was nothing short of withdrawal symptoms to realize that there is a lot else going on out there in the big world. The sole reference was by my daughter who had requested that I bring her an absentee ballot to vote in this her first presidential race. (Obtaining that ballot from our local election officials was worse than trying to deal with the Italian trains, but that's another story.) She did not, however, wish to discuss her vote, nor did any of her fellow students. Poor form. We could learn a bit from our ex-pats.

The most sage bit of wisdom I learned while traveling came from a conversation I overheard in a café in Siena. This line should be stamped on T-shirts, needlepointed on pillows, and thoroughly ingested by everyone after this election. With the proverbial stiff upper lip, a British matron was chastising her complaining husband over lunch, "We are NOT lost a 'tall, my dear. One simply wanders on."

The summer of 2001 I join my daughter in New York where she is pursuing one of her dreams and living out one of mine. She has a college internship at Forbes magazine. I close a deal, wing it to the Big Apple to take her to places she's dying to go. We play and shop a bit at Saks. We eat at Windows on the World at the Trade Center, where I feel slightly queasy at the height and that elevator ride. A month later 9/11 occurs, and all I can picture is people in that lobby. The Twin Towers were near my daughter's summer job subway station. Shaken she comes home from college, where the streets of Dallas are eerily silent. I have lived through two Kennedy and the King assasinations. I've known guys who went to 'Nam. I've already had my own personal 9/11s during college. But this rocks her soul. Her older brothers are concerned about not only the country but also their futures and careers. This is not the bravado of the teenagers who wanted to kick butt in Desert Storm but the concern of mature young men looking at their futures. Several of my real estate deals are on hold, and I face the fear of a nation as well as financial fear. We learn of friends of friends who lose loved ones. It's a sobering autumn.

October 2001, *Homeland Security (Yikes!)*

The Office of Homeland Security. Yikes. It sounds like something out of a Kafka novel or an old Cold War Soviet spy movie. Like a lot of Americans I'm not sleeping all that well these days. How's a body to "resume normal living" when every morning, noon, and night we're all checking the news to see if there are any more horror stories. Nothing feels too secure with anthrax spores floating around, enraged Arabs in places with unpronounceable names burning American flags on the nightly news, and airports resembling armed camps.

Some government agency has already given a grant to Hollywood screenwriters to concoct terrorist scripts so we can think like crazies and get one step ahead of the game. I'm not sure that's the best use of taxpayer funds. You could get any group of college kids drinking beer in a bar or some really, really smart unemployed people to do the same thing for free. Even I can come up with some stuff. All you have to do is think about how to create panic and disrupt the economy in such a way that American capitalism will implode. Don't worry about schools or churches. Think oil refineries, the Commodities Exchange, Microsoft, etc.

As this is going on my widowed mother, who has moved Ft. Worth to be near my doctor brother is diagnosed as terminal. I do my best to give her the comfort she never gave me, because I have come a long way baby. She gave me life; she gave me a great education. Be grateful for what you got, not what you did not. Still it is emotionally exhausting.

October 2001, *Hospice (From Ground Zero to across town)*

Death is death. It happens to us all regardless of our beliefs, faith, convictions, character or lack of any. What differs for each human life is the living of it, the leaving of it. Despite the inevitability of death it can still shock. So many of the families of the victims could not bring themselves to "give up hope" for weeks after the catastrophe. In deference to their anguish they are still referred to as "missing" rather than dead. When death comes without warning it can leave us disoriented and overwhelmed. And so the workers at the site, those who shovel through the rubble at Ground Zero at first looking for life, now trying to find any shred of identifying a dead person are heroes. Many lost fellow emergency co-workers. It is right that we honor those whose service is dangerous, emotionally draining, grim, and helpful. We need not travel to Ground Zero to find them. I, for one, need only go into the next room, where a hospice worker is changing my dying mother's diaper.

My mother has lived seven years longer than the Biblical three score and ten. Along with her heart disease the last few years, she has also battled depression and fear of her demise. Hers was a conflicted life. Once cancer entered into her system she came to resignation. While death may be normal, it is not easy. Neither is the slow ending and breaking down of a body. We have called in hospice.

I marvel at how the home nurses, ordinary women, do such extraordinary things with such kindness and practicality. Changing diapers, giving sponge baths, swabbing her mouth for oral hygiene, turning her to avoid bedsores; none of these are pleasant tasks and require all of us there. Despite our best efforts with lovely lotions and flowers, there is the pungent odor of a life ending; her breathing and groans are difficult to hear.

Yet Alicia, Guadenia, Lucinda and others leave their jobs as health care professionals to spend another eight hours helping our family with tasks that would repel most. These people will not be heralded in concert halls yet they are no less heroic in their jobs than many who risk their lives.

As I thank Alicia, not knowing if this will be her last shift and wondering how she does this job, she gave me a hug and whispered, "Honey we all got mamas."

My concerned daughter insists I need something wagging its tail after this fall of misery. It's nice for her too. Happiness is a warm puppy.

December 2001, *Puppy Love (Gotta redeem 2001)*

It's the Christmas season. Sorta. The beat goes on. It's been proclaimed officially that we're now in a recession, like we didn't all know it with all the layoffs. Suicide bombers in Israel, battling forces in Kandahar, anthrax letters still under investigation…add on to that scene the death of George Harrison, the "quiet" Beatle, and it's been a bummer of a fall. What's a body to do to get in the Christmas spirit in this sober year of muted cheerfulness?

Cocoon. Go home and surround yourself with family, friends, a blazing hearth, a pot of stew simmering on the stove, and soft music. Stay real. I'm so real that I can't stay awake. That's because I've been up for the third straight night under the influence of three pounds of a wiggling white muff that now keeps me chained to the home front. Santa came a little early with my new puppy. After all the transition, violence, and death, which included that of my surviving parent, I decided it was time to do something I swore as an empty nester I'd never do: get a dog. After raising a family and an assortment of pets, and developing a career, I thought that houseplants were almost more than I wanted to care for. With doggies it's goodbye freedom, hello house. Alas, my kids convinced me I needed a wagging tail at the end of the day.

So how, on December 1st, did I end up driving back from East Texas with another male Bichon Frise who ended up with the name Baci ("Kisses" in Italian after my daughter's Italian semester abroad)? Well, like of much of my life, things didn't turn out as envisioned. Within 24 hours I blearily wondered what had possessed me to get back into vaccinations, blotting up "accidents," running to the pet store countless times a day (in Christmas traffic no less) to pick up food, toys, dishes, brushes and all the myriad paraphernalia that no pet lover can live without. Plus he needed a hernia repair. The incredible expense of owning a well-heeled dog came flooding back. Needless to say whenever Baci finally takes a nap so do I. Who knows if I'll find the time to get out Christmas cards.

But last night, as I bundled up with a pooped out white mop gazing up with adoring black liquid eyes and flipped on "America at War" I knew exactly why I had my little Baci, the new man in my life. In times of death and transition and in the spirit of Advent, there is nothing quite like new life. Who needs jewelry or clothes or that new (shudder) piece of technology under a tree? The

Beatles were right. All you need is love.

December 2001, *Holidays (What a difference a year makes)*

What a difference a year makes! This time last year holiday family tables had more to quibble about than whether to serve mashed potatoes or sweet potatoes. Whole families got indigestion and lost the holiday spirit debating chads, dimpled ballots, undervotes and overvotes, and who would be president. Just saying Al Gore or George Bush could send Uncle George or Gramps into a tirade. Now we are a nation under attack involved in a war half way round the world with people and places we'd never even heard of before Labor Day. Jalalabad, Kabul, Osama Bin Laden, the Taliban, Al Qaeda are all household names. Yet this will not be a year to debate politics as usual, even foreign policy around the turkey. Since 9/11, history has changed and the holiday spirit is remarkably muted. Despite the havoc that has been wreaked on our incredibly prosperous, free, open society, our suffering has brought us many blessings. Blessings for which we can be thankful.

Because our public buildings were attacked and innocent victims were horrendously murdered, we have come together as one American people no longer divided by hyphenated ethnic groups, race, gender, color or age. We have renewed our patriotism, protected our public buildings, and regained respect for those in authority. We have gone from a nation who watched Survivor to becoming survivors. We have matured.

So I thought, and perhaps for a while we did. Until we fragmented. "If winter comes can spring be far behind?" Not published in the paper but an email (that new technology) I sent to my sorority sisters for our 30th.

Fwd: *The Sisterhood, Reunion* Date: May 6:45 AM

Ok here's the deal. I want everyone at 5 o'clock on Friday of reunion weekend at Rotier's with cell phones. I'll buy the first round. Send your husbands to the pinball machines. It's my birthday and I want some celebrants. Everyone is to bring the name, possibly photo, and phone number of one eligible bachelor from your hometown. The cutest pledge class that ever was will then survey these guys and after several beers, the one we drink cute will be the guy who gets a group phone call to set up the blind date that can't be any worse than the ones I've had. Some requirements:

<u>Not a guy who has been reincarnated from several lives</u>... last week's date had been at Antietam and a Nazi spy in WW2. You can't make this stuff up.

<u>Employed.</u> Have been out with every guy driving his net worth in Texas. Don't want to do the same from the guys in your state.

<u>Reasonably attractive.</u> At this point must weigh under 300 pounds.

<u>Somewhat articulate.</u> Doesn't end sentences with "at" like "So where's your house at?" True, I live in Texas.

<u>No small kids.</u> I've raised three and don't need to do any more.

<u>Hygiene.</u> Have been out with a guy with a booger on his nose, one who had horrific BO, a guy with stains on his pants. I realize this might indicate a wife, but basic hygiene.

<u>Age.</u> Limit is about ten years. Have been out with a 70 year old trying to pass for 60 who didn't know who the Rolling Stones were. Not enough meds or white wine on the planet for that.

<u>Single.</u> Don't do "separated but confused."

Ok, ladies I realize I'm being picky but I'm a Theta after all. You've got a month or so to get creative. Let's get cracking. Theta love, Zoe "Honey, I don't know anybody I'd want you to go out with; there's just nobody normal." The universal lament.

My daughter is graduating so my nest is truly empty now as she job hunts.

August 2002, *Womanly Changes (My daughter's choices, the new normal)*

"Here's my daughter's e-mail address. She has friends working in San Francisco." My daughter is off to San Francisco next week to chase a job lead, but she is lukewarm because she knows no one in that city. Hence my friend's e-mail tip to hook her up. Job leads are too hard to come by these days. I tucked my social acquaintance's slip of paper into my purse and marveled. We were doing what women have always done: sipping lady-like drinks and nibbling on party food while oohing and aahing over a happy young lady's wedding shower gifts. A mutual friend's 27-year-old daughter is getting married and we are initiating her into the rite of passage—pretty linens and kitchen utensils. Yet we have also just done what men have always done on the golf course; we are networking and mentoring. The new normal.

My daughter is not getting married. At 22 and

about to graduate from college she's much too young, never mind that I was engaged and had been a bridesmaid half a dozen times at her age. It's a hackneyed cliché, but times have changed, and the main reason is that our daughters have opportunities that our sons have which were never available to us mothers. A generation ago getting married at 27 would be narrowly averting old maid status. Most nice girls went to college to get a pleasant liberal arts degree that would be useful at dinner parties and to meet an eligible young man. If we didn't begin procreating immediately, we taught school or worked for Daddy or a close friend's Daddy. While that scenario still occurs, it's almost quaint today. We took menial jobs in order to help promote our husbands' careers until the babies came. True, things began to change in the 70s, but the South was the last bastion of that change. My friends who ended up in power careers did so by default because they had not found "Mr. Right" or serendipitously because they had some job experience at a time when pressure was being brought to bear to hire women.

It used to be that a young woman got to New York or Chicago as she followed her husband's career. Now young women go to college to get on a career track. Upon graduation, they either pick an interesting city and then seek employment or follow a job offer if it's in an interesting city. Some years DC is "hot," other years it's Atlanta or LA. New York is always "in."

My sorority sister in Atlanta, a former schoolteacher, sighed over the phone as she kept her daughter's grandchild while the child's mother was making medical rounds at Emory.

"I'm just a little jealous of her."

Her daughter is finishing her medical residency.

My most Catholic friend, who is the mother of many, admitted at a coffee last week, "I sometimes wonder what life would have been like if we'd had our daughters' lives...then I just repress that thought."

My friend who champions James Dobson's *Focus on the Family* and avows motherhood as a woman's highest calling, nevertheless, has confided that she is slightly envious of her daughter's freedom in her West Coast job and life. We all want to be mother of the bride and grandmothers, but we want so much for our daughters to follow their dreams and live a little before settling down. If I ask fellow empty-nester moms if they wouldn't like to be 22 again, having the opportunities our daughters have, to a woman, each gets a wistful look and murmurs, "You bet."

By now I've downscaled again to a bungalow not in the Bubble, right around the corner from where I lived as a Parkland resident's wife for 15 times the price. I like this familiar neighborhood, and I'm simplifying. No more Christmas trees and trying to maintain the silver, crystal and china thing. The streamlining, clearing out, adjusting to life after kids phase has arrived.

Thanksgiving 2002, *(Food rules exhausting, just eat out)*

Thanksgiving is the American tribal rite when animosities are suspended between various members of ethnic, political, and gender related groups and personality types, namely families, to recognize that they all share one common heritage; namely eating turkey. This is the only holiday that centers around food; thus the meal is crucial. While other holiday rites might include beef, quail, goose, baked ham, or traditional religious foods, the kindergarten teachers of America, for as far back as anyone can remember, had every school child drawing pictures of Pilgrims and Indians feasting on turkey. This is probably because kids can trace their hands to resemble turkey feathers and cut and paste to create wonderful art projects. So turkey is now standard fare, and appliance manufacturers have complied by designing ovens in every kitchen to accommodate Big Bird. When Norman Rockwell sketched the Thanksgiving family turkey scene for the cover of the *Saturday Evening Post,* we were all obliged to re-enact the scene.

Before the iconic bird can even be purchased, there is the critical decision of how to cook the thing. There are now turkey hotlines, Internet sites, cooking shows as well as grannies' cookbooks for advice. So adamant are some people about their food preferences that there is really only one thing to do, which is what I as a single mother now do every year. Go out to eat and give thanks.

My middle son is marrying, a destination wedding at his old alma mater. It is off limits to write about my adult kids, they have instructed, so my columns are kvetching about jury duty, traffic, government spending, air travel, computer crashes, atrocious grammar, horrible fashions, local politics. Still, I make oblique references when I can.

January 2003, *Mother of the Groom...The Dress*

What are you wearing? It's the universal greeting of women of all ages, starting at about age four. This is hardwired along with the Y chromosome into female

DNA. When attending any event, all a guy wants to know is whether is requires a tie or not, and hopefully, not. Then it's just a question of golf shirt and khakis or jeans and boots. Period. Never do men sit around during a round of golf or at a sports bar and debate whether a double-breasted or three button blazer is a better look at a party. It's just not part of their conversational pattern.

Whether it's a dinner party, a brunch, the prom, or a seventh grade cotillion, females will initiate a small flurry of phone calls to check out what other females are wearing. It's important to be similar but never the same. This is called having "fashion sense." For me, I usually have the fashion police (my daughter) phoning to beg me not buy anything until she can shop with me. Ok so I hate to shop. This is why I'll never be a native Texan. ("Here, Mom try this. It will give you the illusion of a waist.")

We are experiencing a family wedding. Being part of the baby boomer, empty-nester generation, so are most of my friends. Because weddings involve showers, parties, brunches, and even the wedding ceremony, this necessitates several wardrobe purchases. This, in turn, requires several lunches with friends to discuss these things.

"Have you gotten your Dress?" is at the heart of

the matter. Convention dictates that Mother of the Bride has first choice on dress color. As Mother of the Groom I'm working off of "periwinkle." As my father used to say about the groom's mother, her job was to "wear beige and shut up." (I'm sort of there. Mauve is close to beige.) Lucky guys. All they have to do is wear a black tuxedo. Period.

It takes a village to come up with The Dress. It seems there are specialty stores for this sort of thing. It's important to make sure you don't have the same dress as all the other mothers of the brides and grooms whose wedding you're attending. It's also nice to have a dress that "moves, has forgiveness," photographs well, and is even flattering. This must be done months and months in advance and can cost as much as a trip to Europe ("investment dressing").

Finally, it must be able to be altered to whatever shifting mid-life body shape you happen to be at the time of the Event. The dress must be critiqued by an inner circle. Is it too fussy, too wintry or summery, appropriate for the time of day or night, would it clash with the bridesmaids or bride's mother, and of paramount consideration is whether or not it can it be cut off or ever worn again. Of course, women with daughters are veterans at this.

We've done bridesmaid and professional dressing for our daughters, rush and prom dresses, cotillion and party dresses, in fact, it goes back to poodle skirts, even Christening gowns. Looking for the holy grail of The Dress is a girl thing. It's just sometimes I wish I were a guy.

2003 Press release: "Local realtor named Vice President for top performance."

Just in time to help pay for weddings. It's so hard to earn and keep, so my anger at the economy infects a lot of articles. I feel so overtaxed with not only income tax, high property and sales tax, but also self-employment tax. This whole Wall Street culture is infuriating. I pay my bills on time, stay out of debt with a perfect credit score, live frugally. Just about five years before the big crash, I unleash.

September 2003, *Indispensible? Greed on Wall Street*

You know the definition of indispensable don't you? Get a bucket of water, stick your arm in it; take it out. If the water stays parted you're indispensable. Dick Grasso's not. The day after he "resigned" the NYSE he supposedly regulated jumped 100 points. Apparently the 140 million bucks he was awarded by his Board to regulate the New York Stock Exchange didn't need his expensive prowess to survive and thrive. That's a hefty sum for a job that, until very recently, was largely an honorarium, done by men out of *noblesse oblige*. (This hefty chunk of change was to pay a man who produced nothing, provided jobs to no one, and was in bed with the people he was supposed to regulate.) Everyone is quick to point out he did nothing wrong except to have restrained little during hard times. His Board members were men who themselves were paid such sums for running their businesses and voted to give him such largesse. How have we come to the place in history where the men who run corporate America often line their pockets with obscene compensation packages, while running their corporations into the ground and laying off workers in the process? We have returned to the Age of the Robber Barons. Whatever happened to "Everything in Moderation?" Whatever happened to ethical leadership? No wonder there's such a resurgence of biographies on the founding fathers, who had moral leadership and principals unrelated to crass greed and power.

The formula for creating a dysfunctional family has been adapted by corporate America. ***Secrets***. Enron and Anderson and WorldCom and Merrill were rife with back room deals by arrogant CEO's and management accountable to no one. ***Mixed Messages.*** "We're a team" when corporations were run by autocratic chiefs who surrounded themselves with boards paid by "hush money" to rubber stamp greedy bonuses while turning a blind eye to cooked books ***Favoritism.*** Cronies of CEO's were shoveled business or insider information or warned to unload stock while the nuts and bolt employees were left to fend for themselves. CEO's abound, who feel that the companies they run are their personal fiefdoms created for their own profit, while squandering the most important corporate asset—the human asset.

The people who put their time and energy, which is their life, into a day-to-day job trying to work with as much dignity and effort as possible have often been betrayed by greedy American Pharaohs. Ken Lay, who gave generously to charity and the arts (with corporate funds) thought of himself as a good guy. He isn't. His name is Legion. Merrill Lynch is bullish on America, which means its own upper level management, while screwing its investors. Anderson counted on its respectable name to get away with aiding and abetting the great Enron Loot. WorldCom "lost" a couple of billion dollars on their books, which somehow enhanced the lifestyle of management. I grow weary of hearing that corporate wrongdoing "may not have been illegal" although it was probably unethical. Say what?

The only way to restore confidence and moderation in corporate America is to begin with regulating the Boards and CEO's of Big Business. The rationalization that these obscene compensation packages are the only way to attract and keep talent is absurd. Get out that bucket of water. There's younger, cheaper talent right behind those guys. And the billions in savings could hire the workers needed to stimulate this economy.

In five years substitute Big Business for Big Banks for those phony mortgages and CDO's. Am proud to be with an ethical firm.

Fall 2003, *Tap Dancing (Come on lady, lighten up)*

"And five, six, seven, eight…heel, ball, shuffle, change, flap, flap dig…" It's the warm up drill that gets my adrenalin going, makes me giggle, and has me reverting to my childhood fantasy years. I've just joined a beginning class for old, fat ladies who want to tap dance. Well, not so old and not so fat but the Rockettes we're not. In fact, some of us are a little spastic. Still, there was nothing else to do after seeing the movie *Chicago*. If Richard Gere and Renee Zellweger could learn how to do it, then so could I. Not that the point is to compete with movie stars or even the other tappers in my class. It's just about having a little fun.

The pros make tapping look so easy. Trust me it isn't. It takes practicing the same little movement over and over until it's a reflex instead of a thought process. Sort of like learning a second language. Tap dancing is a metaphor for life: the individual steps aren't hard; it's the transitions that are difficult. But put on shoes with those little pieces of metal and your feet just start moving. It's impossible to worry about Iraq, income taxes, the kids, business, irritating people while hopping around on feet sounding like cap guns.

Everybody needs a little virtual tap dancing: what makes you feel like you're playing like you did as a kid. Making a mess. Being noisy. Feeling free. That might be playing the bongos, getting muddy in the garden, pitching pots, finger painting, making a mess in the kitchen while whipping up a soufflé. Whatever makes you laugh out loud or giggle. In serious times and downturns it's that much more important. Heel, ball, shuffle, change.

All my life I had looked younger than my age. I was short (petite is the word I'm groping for) but all of sudden I did not. Maybe it was when my daughter came into my bathroom as I was stepping out of the shower and gagged. "Cover up, you've got cellulite!" Ah, a true Dallas Parkie. Also I live in Dallas where looking good is the never-ending story. What to do?

Fall 2003, *Natural Beauty or Plastic Surgery? (Looks are exhausting)*

While lunching with "the girls," a lady I had not seen in awhile stopped by the table. She looked terrific.

"She's a natural beauty" one of my lunch bunch sighed.

The silence that followed was leaden as we all took personal inventory. We are, after all, at the half-century mark, a few were now grannies. There's no such thing as a natural beauty after a certain age. Without whipping out calculators, it was nevertheless obvious that mental calculations were going on. How did we stack up? This gal wasn't a classic Grace Kelly beauty. She just looked great. She was way beyond vitamins and exercise. Living in Dallas can be exhausting. Competitive body maintenance is the norm.

She was toned. This means hundreds of hours of physical fitness, probably with a personal trainer. Weights, yoga, Pilates? Which was it? Flesh fights gravity for women of a certain age. Where had she been nipped and tucked? Tummy, thighs, eyes, face? Who was her doctor? She had managed to avoid that wind tunnel, lizard look if it had been the face. Her skin glowed. Was it Retin A, Botox, collagen injections, laser resurfacing, chemical or vegetable peels, facials, or a great line of make-up? Or a combination of some of each? She looked "clean." Probably half of her body had been waxed, from legs to eyebrows to bikini line. No doubt she'd had her spider web capillaries collapsed on her face and legs. Probably her dermatologist had burned off any age spots. Those sheer nails didn't fool anybody. Definitely manicured, probably tips or wraps. Without looking it was a safe bet she was pedicured as well. She was "healthy" looking. No doubt she had been to the tanning salon or maybe one of those places which sprays on a tan. It was also entirely possible she'd just gotten back from some fabulous island trip or a spa week. Her smile was radiant. Had she done clear braces? At the very least she'd bleached those pearly whites. Her hair? Well, she lives in Dallas so naturally she had gleaming blonde highlights. But she had a great cut–

simple with movement. Who was her stylist? Her eyes sparkled. Probably a lash dye but maybe she had tinted contacts too. She'd probably been with a nutritionist, taken the right mix of vitamins and herbs and had given up red meat. Her casual clothes were coral and lime, this year's colors, so she'd put in her hours of shopping. Her accessories were simple and correct: this year it's beading. Her makeup was minimal, which means she'd applied it carefully in a magnifying mirror after first moisturizing with some exotic "wrinkle minimizing" cream.

I figured this natural look cost at least ten thousand dollars but probably double that. It involved hundreds of hours of hard work. "Great genes" one of my friends intoned. We all forced smiles as we dug into our salads.

Summer 2004, *Weddings and Love on my Mind*

Call me romantic but I love weddings. Big and splashy, small and intimate, weddings in gardens, ballrooms, cathedrals, living rooms or wherever, if they're serious commitments. (Not the ones on Ferris wheels sponsored by some radio station.) Watching the merging of two lives is a drama not to be missed. Every couple tries to imprint their own unique stamp or fingerprint on the nuptials. No two marriages are any more alike than two snowflakes. Whether there are trumpets, string quartets, or a simple guitar makes no difference. It is the simple sincerity of the sentiments being expressed, the purity of the promises being made that make any wedding a passion play. It is the melding of two distinct clans. It is always fraught with tension, stress, but the possibility of great love. It is that hope which keeps us boxing up trivets and bon bon dishes and tossing prayers and rose petals on two infatuated hearts. It is very much more than a "piece of paper."

And what tribal rites occur! Granny grump who grouses over the décolletage of the bridesmaids, or Uncle Rascal who always has three too many, the inevitable *faux pas* of a forgotten toast, or lost suitcase, or disappearing studs. There is one side of the aisle warily surveying the other side's "people," yet when the couple gaze into each other's eyes and say "I do" the Republicans lie down with the Democrats, the Hatfields with the McCoys, the ritzy with the simple, the Southerners with the Yankees. Even those families who are already friends have the inevitable alcoholic uncle, crazy aunt, loud-mouthed brother-in-law, or obnoxious toddlers.

So there can be an incredible amount of preparation for The Event. But why not? It is, after all, the declaration of the casseroling of two lives, and the hope that love changes the universe of each of us forever.

Not so my oldest, my maverick. He elopes without fanfare.

February 2006, *Valentine's Day* (*Even for one, although I was flying a new beau under the radar.*)

Valentine's Day is upon us. If you didn't realize it just turn on the radio or TV and listen to the barrage of Dr. Laura's or Dr. Phil's dispensing advice about love, or go online into a chat room. What seems to come out of all this endless analyzing is that men are lunatics while women are merely nuts. Men always want to be a woman's first love, while women want men to be their last romance. For women, romance is an occupation, for men a preoccupation. After the initial courtship phase, women want a commitment. Women want to change their man, men want their women not to change. Men go to bed and wake up looking about the same, while women deteriorate over night, get depressed and go shopping. Men go hunting. The dailyness of life begins to bleed the romance out of love; people get bored so then along comes Valentine's. It's a day to make amends, a chance to rekindle old feelings, or woo a love interest.

The initiation into the mysteries of coquetry begins at a tender age, usually preschool, when lassies adorn shoeboxes with doilies, glitter, and tin foil, then spend days making or picking out cards. For little boys their moms usually end up doing the hard lifting here.

As an aside for those in the world of singledom take heart! Put on *Sergeant Pepper's Lonely Heart Club Band* and clean out that shoebox with unrequited love items. Those letters, or snapshots or an old tear stained diary. Make a little bonfire and open that bottle of bubbly. Finally, a heads up for all the men in relationships or those who want to start one. Get to the florist before the flowers run out. Make restaurant reservations early. She'll be too busy picking out just the right card.

Spring 2006, *The Granny Diaries (I want to join that club)*

I am a bit jealous of my friends who are Mimi's, Cece's, Gigi's, Kaki's, and all the other modern grandmother names they so proudly bear. Nobody is Granny or Meemaw any more. And the guys are all Dude, or Big Bob, or Pal, or something a lot more swinging than Gramps or Pawpaw. Despite the fact that none of us can quite believe we're old enough to be that grandparenting age, I was in a generation of women who graduated and soon after had babies. Even though waiting longer, our babies are now young professionals having their own. How I want some! But the equipment! So much for a high chair, play pen and stroller.

I recently changed a client's baby while she perused her contract, and I was amazed. The paper diapers are now as soft as the cloth ones of my days, when disposable diapers felt like cardboard. I was instructed to put the wad into a contraption sort of like a Venus flytrap, which sucked it into a tight ball. When filled this "genie" would then shoot the cannonballs into the garbage pail. When I deposited her princess into a baby seat I almost dropped her from the jolt. It was vibrating like the "magic fingers" on a Barcalounger.

I've witnessed a young family carting gear that looked like a cross-country move. Long gone are simple diaper bags, and heaven forbid you don't have hand sanitizer and electronics in your purse. Does this go hand in hand with competitive parenting?

Each generation thinks it will improve upon the parenting model. Hadn't my own been self-congratulatory because we gave "time-outs" instead of spankings? That we pureed baby food instead of using processed? Well, at least for the first baby that is. Hadn't we introduced disposable diapers? But this generation has grown up on the Internet in chat rooms, and the young mommies come to grandmamma with lists of instructions backed by studies. One told me her son tried to show her how to diaper his daughter.   "It's remarkably similar to how I diapered your sister," she deadpanned.

Another rolls her eyes over a daughter-in-law's insistence on keeping a poop and pee diary whenever she babysits.

A friend, while strolling a grandchild in the neighborhood giving her ward a cookie sighed,

"I like them so much more before they can tattle on you. The mothers have so many rules now, and treats never make the list."

So when my friend kept her new grandchild, she showed me two single spaced typed pages of instructions from her daughter with everything from numbers for poison control to instructions to "Call 911 if he chokes. She rolled her eyes. "He'll need THREE naps and don't let him have them in the car. Green food only, NO FRUIT; he gets that next month. Do NOT let the dog near him, and only let him play with his sterilized toys that don't have lead."

As soon as her daughter departed Mamie just handed me her crying grandson. While I tried to figure out which hi-tech contraption to place him in, she threw a quilt on the floor. Then she tossed him her keys and smiled as the dog licked his feet.

June 2006, *Commence to Mature (Bragging and Complaining)*

Twice in the last week I swallowed a lump in my throat as my daughter graduated from law school and my second son from dental school. In each case the introit was impressive with trumpeters, faculty wearing colorful regalia of gowns and mortarboards with the array of bars and stripes signifying their own academic accomplishments. These ceremonies hark back to medieval times with the rise of scholasticism and are the wrap up the training they have given to young professionals to commence their careers.

When, however, did graduations devolve into pep rallies? My first clue times had changed was the audience dress code or rather lack of it. The people sitting in Hawaiian shirts, flip flops, cowboy hats which were never removed, clearly had never been to a performance in the Symphony Hall, that was the venue for one event.

The law school crowd was even worse, maybe because it was outdoors. People talked on their cell phones during the Senator's address, used foghorns when their graduate walked across the stage, blew kazoos and in one case rang cowbells. Even the SEC banned those at football games. Maybe we could get the SEC to regulate the manners of the families of graduating professionals and the students themselves. That is, if they want to be taken seriously in their vocations.

May 2007, *PO'd (Finally here comes the bride)*

While braving the monsoons we have been having this spring, I took the carefully plastic wrapped creamy envelopes into a remote post office that carried wedding stamps, as my branch was out. Just our luck that there was to be another rate hike before the wedding and the new stamps weren't out yet. Would the old ones work? Would we need to add an ugly non-wedding supplemental stamp on these vellum packets? As the official MOB (mother of the bride) of a young lady wrapping up law school, I said I'd handle this although, unlike me who had virtually no input with my mother when I married, my daughter is the decision maker in this very understated, traditional upcoming event. We did not splurge on the newest craze of personalized wedding stamps with a photo of the bride and groom. We did, however, splurge on heavy stationery for engraved invitations and used a calligrapher for addressing since my writing is illegible and she is too busy. Were they too heavy with the reply card or too large for a regular LOVE stamp? The supervisor came out and said she had no idea. Say what? Since they were going out of the country. Huh? She pointed to the word "Columbia." The elegant script read Washington, District of Columbia for at least a dozen invitations. When I told her it was not Bogota but the city where our president lived, she just smiled and shrugged. How many of these prized possessions would actually arrive at their destination? Now I'm PO'd.   I've just been Post Officed.

My kids were all graduates, in healthy relationships, had managed to avoid drugs, had productive jobs. It was done, and they were my heroes. Thank goodness their parents did not derail them. All those gray hairs from worrying about everything from ADD to grades, car wrecks, broken hearts, broken bones was just unnecessary.

One night at steak dinner, we laughed over my being the guinea pig in dental school, where my son was practicing making a mouth mold (mine) and came out and shot a photo while I was stuck, mouth clamped open, with goo dripping down my chin. His classmates found this hilarious. My bemused daughter shook her head remembering our trip to DC in sweltering heat, when my forgotten meds had to be overnighted as my hot flashes seemed worse than labor.

"You were a mess, Mom!"

When I thought I was regaling my oldest son at this, his birthday dinner about how, as a toddler, he had finger-painted all over the walls with poop from his diaper, he "regaled" me back by sharing how he had sneaked the car out past an elderly sitter to paintball stop signs in middle school, when we were out of town. This led to a few other undetected escapades. Gulp. We can only remember what we know. It takes constant re-editing with new information, and we all have different memories in the same story.

Adults all. I helped them get under contract with their first houses. They were launched. My turn! I'm ready for the rest of life, the best for which the first was made. Now I'm the one driving a green convertible with the wind blowing in my hair.

TURBO SPIN

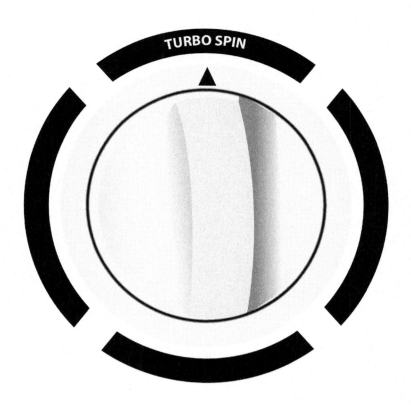

NORMAL'S JUST A CYCLE ON A WASHING MACHINE

Part Five: Turbo Spin

2004

In which we meet online; whirlwind dating ensues as he pursues ardently. We laugh a lot. I have fun; my shrink warns not a good fit: "different tribes."

2005

In which he falls in love with me and buys his all-important ranch as a family retreat to assuage enmeshed adult daughters.

2006

In which he proposes and recants after daughters' rants, then begs for another chance: drama and melodrama. An emotional rollercoaster.

2007

In which we pull the trigger and elope in Santa Fe. His initial elation swings to immediate emotional breakdown under daughters' tirades; we start couple's counseling.

2008

In which he has health issues, money issues, family issues, and I peddle hard, so I won't fail at remarriage. Can't write or do business; he reneges on buying a house per our pre-nup.

2009

In which I finally blow up at the saboteurs, and he begins a downhill spiral of anger, negativity and criticism (at me, not them).

2010

In which I realize this chaos is permanent. I am trapped in King Lear, but we are taking a lot of cruises. I gain weight.

2011

In which I just try to keep people around us for civility when we do see each other; and I try to figure out in therapy why I've recreated the tumult of my family of origin.

2012

In which divorce is final. Flew it under the radar. Always lived in our own homes in different counties, and with his 60 page pre-nup, nothing much changes. Well, maybe my self esteem. And I lose weight.

(Poor) Me: I guess I failed at marriage...again. And I was warned.

(Best) Self: No you did not. The relationship failed despite your best efforts; you gotta have hope.

Once again my life seems like bad country song. Both my exes live in Texas. So I go visit friends in Tennessee (and other places.)

Sound bytes to others: Pieces of the puzzle didn't fit. Family issues. Family secrets. Never got under the same roof. Never got to normal.

Q: (always) "What were you thinking dating online?"

A: Sigh. The days of little dinner parties with people setting you up are just so over. I enjoy male company; I got tired of singledom. This town goes two by two. With age, dates were fewer and further apart. Friends encouraged me to get with the new millennium. I wanted an adventure. Worked for some hadn't it?

After the online experience of what can euphemistically be called awkward Starbucks'

encounters and one mismatched marriage, I'm offline. Or as the saying goes, "be careful what you wish for."

Just because a relationship ends doesn't mean it was without value. I may not ever understand the whys in some, only the hows; but everyone has the free will to take different paths on the journey. I don't think any of the pain I encountered in relationships was the original intention of that person. My wounds were only in proportion to how much I had invested. With every rupture I had to look deep inside myself.

I still like men. And women. Especially children. But most importantly, me.

GENTLE

Part Six: Gentle Wash

January 2014, *Sacred Spaces*

There are places in our lives that often become sacred spaces, where there is the overwhelming feeling of something holy. For some it is a special tree by a creek, or a spot in a backyard garden. For me, battlefield cemeteries have this feel: Vicksburg, Normandy, the 9/11 Memorial. Some churches or chapels have resonated with me; the Cathedral at Chartres, a tiny chapel at Saint Michael and All Angels, also a beach near where I grew up…but always a newborn nursery, where the infants, "so fresh from God" as Dickens once said, lay experiencing life outside the womb. Newborns are certainly common, yet each birth is a miracle, each uncommonly distinct. Infants are as unique as snowflakes. Sadly, not all newborns are as welcome as others. There is the mild disappointment of yet another child of the same gender when "changing flavors" was desired, or the rejected child of an addicted mother, the babes who come forth with obvious abnormalities, which portend a foreshortened life or a life filled with challenges. But it was only last week that I entered a birthing room at Margot Perot Hospital, gazing at a mother, father and newborn…a sacred trinity. My son, his wife and their son. All was perfection and joy, just as it was when I was there 38 years ago in that same place.

Soon I was inhaling the fragrance, nuzzling the unblemished skin, stroking the crown of velvet fuzz on my new grandchild. Embracing this one-hour-old package swaddled in blankets was akin to cradling a warm loaf of bread. Large for our family at nearly eight and a half pounds, yet startling how very small.

This, my fifth grandchild, was nevertheless my first grandson. Would we have loved another ballerina princess? Of course. Yet this little man was "carrying on the family name" that would have died out, which in the Deep South is still something. Actually, despite the fact that feudal primogeniture has fallen by the much-needed wayside, the desire for a male child at some point still pervades much of the world. It's not just in China where girl baby infanticide has been a problem, or in the parts of the Middle East or other patriarchal societies where women are regarded as chattel. Even in America where we adore our daughters, there is some secret implicit desire in many families to sire a male.

Gender was not a surprise in this day and age unlike the arrival of my firstborn male nearly forty years ago, when I produced the little man who would "carry on the family name." Still not sure why this undercurrent of maleness persists. Perhaps it is just history which is ever changing.

Like all proud grannies, I posted his visage on Facebook and emailed a dozen friends. Then I spent the next hour doing what families do. I tried to remember if he looks like his father did at birth, if he has my family's mouth or nose, or coloring. Did he have our feet, fingers, and hairline? Both sides produced old photo albums to jog our memories. I thrilled at his every coo, mewl and yawn, watched breathlessly as his eyes fluttered, and he frantically searched for his thumb while making sucking sounds. There it was, his first smile. A dream...or gas? Watching his little spindly legs unbend as he was cuffed with an ankle monitor so he would be protected as ours was akin to watching a fawn rise on wobbly legs.

An infant is endlessly fascinating to the birth family, and despite all good wishes, less so to others. Among the welcoming emails responses, it took one fellow granny of boys who wrote "Isn't it amazing how they look like grumpy old men at first, but in a few years become these young studs," to penetrate my fog. I rechecked the photo I had sent out...his eyes were swollen from the drops, his lips puckered and brow furrowed. Still, he was gorgeous. Surveying my bundle of perfection I did not want to fast forward 15 years to those studly years. In the beginning there is only this marvelous innocence. And it is sacred.

A couple of years later

So I pick up the phone to listen to the litany of woes from a tired, sleep deprived mom, my own baby, my daughter. Her new infant son won't sleep, and the colic still won't subside; he needs tubes in his ears. Her little girls won't eat anything but one brand of mac n' cheese and have both nixed fruit; one won't wear anything that doesn't look like a punk rocker to school, and they want to be on iPads all day. They can barely read and now they want to text. The guy didn't show up to fix the stove, which means another night of microwaved junk…

Umm, you had two sets of tubes, your brother one set and asthma, the other one was always getting stitches, you were on special formula the first year, and everything breaks down, I thought but did not say. I smile inwardly while giving my old dog, Baci, his arthritis meds.

"Aaah, honey I wish I lived closer. What you're doing is not practicing law; I know it's tedious even boring, but it's where you want to be right now. Treasure it while you can. The days may seem slow…but the years fly by.

Throughout my life, my favorite prayer has always been, "Dear Lord, surprise me."

He did.

Afterword

Looking back over my life as played out in my newspaper articles, I realize that old bromide that "everything comes out in the wash" isn't so. Some clothes bleed or fade, and others shrink or change shape. The clothes don't always get sorted, the water temperature isn't always adjusted, some pieces just have to be tossed. It doesn't mean they weren't great fits at one time. That other old saw, "everything that goes around comes around" is only sort of true. Those disappointing, untrustworthy, wardrobe malfunctions don't always get their comeuppance. Some stains just set, but they eventually fade. On the other hand, life does keep cycling on. The real wonder is how much we cram into our personal wash loads and how quickly they spin. Without that friction, clothes just wouldn't get clean. Then we pull out our wardrobes and put them back on. Only they're never new again. Sometimes that's better.

For more of Len Bourland's columns go to
www.lenbourland.com
Email lenbourland@gmail.com

Acknowledgements

My gratitude goes to all who assisted me in getting this to print. First my editor Heather McPherson; Jen Leblanc for her invaluable assistance in producing this; Courtney Barrow for her wonderful artwork and book jacket design; Elizabeth Cauthorn and Spike Gillespie for moving me forward; Ellen Westbrook for her copy editing; Wendy Soper McSweeney for her invaluable help in editing, Photolively for formatting, Jim Patterson at Ingram and all those friends who write, who encouraged me to weave my columns into this story, and of course, my children whose lives have always inspired me.

About the Author

Born in New Orleans, Len Persons Bourland lived in Houston, Texas; Sao Paulo, Brazil; Atlanta, Georgia; Nashville, Tennessee; Aix-en-Provence, and Jackson, Mississippi before moving to Dallas, where she has lived for over 40 years. She credits some formidable old ladies at Westminster Prep in Atlanta for her love of language. She holds undergraduate and graduate degrees in history from Vanderbilt and SMU. In addition to writing and teaching, at mid-life Len became a sales vice president in residential real estate. This confluence of cultures and experiences has shaped her humor, which is at once anecdotal and universal.

She continues to wear many hats, but her favorite is that of Lolly to her six grandchildren.

She can be reached at lenbourland@gmail.com.

www.photolively.com